THE RIGHT HON.

LORD HANKEY

P.C., G.C.B., G.C.M.G., G.C.V.O.

LL.D. (Birmingham, Edinburgh, Cambridge), D.LL. (Oxford), F.R.S.

POLITICS

TRIALS

AND

ERRORS

HENRY REGNERY COMPANY

20 WEST JACKSON BOULEVARD, CHICAGO 4,
ILLINOIS

First published 1950

POLITICS, TRIALS
AND ERRORS

LORD HANKEY

CONTENTS

v

INTRODUCTION

WARS usually begin and end in politics. They are preceded by long negotiation, conference, international efforts for peace, threats, cold war, and intolerable strain, culminating in an act of war, with or without formal declaration. At the end of the war, when the result comes in sight, politics are again resumed. The normal course of events for many centuries has then been an Armistice, a Peace Conference, and a Peace Treaty. In World War II, however, exasperated by the aggressions and crimes of their enemies, the Allies adopted a new political technique and announced their intention that they would accept nothing less than the Unconditional Surrender of all their foes and that the guilty, barbarian leaders would be punished. The main object of this book is to examine for the benefit of the present generation and posterity the political results of this breach with tradition. They have been far-reaching in their many ramifications and have led to draconian measures.

My personal reactions were immediate, definite, and sustained. Within a month of the demand for Unconditional Surrender, in an unpublished Appreciation of the war in all its aspects, which I produced every six months and sent to a small but responsible circle, I wrote as follows: ' In the political field the most important and most dubious step is the announcement of the policy of Unconditional Surrender of all our foes. The policy of Unconditional Surrender may be right or wrong. . . . The *announcement* of the policy, however, which Mr. Churchill made clear was the wish of President Roosevelt, is contrary to the old principle of not driving an enemy to desperation, which it is likely to do. . . .' A repetition of that warning in even more emphatic terms in my next Appreciation, September 3, 1943, was followed by these words: ' In the same order of ideas it would be well to lay less emphasis on the trial of War Criminals. . . . The threatening and boastful talk about it tends to prolong the war.' All my subsequent Appreciations developed in ever-increasing detail the dangers of these policies, and I made several speeches in the House of

Lords on the subject, but without noticeably influencing policy.[1]

The last of the series, dated March 3, 1945, included the following passage: ' Whatever other effects the allied threats about the trials of war criminals may have had, they have done nothing to help the unfortunate victims of German sadism and Japanese barbarity. From the Baltic Provinces, Central France, Belgium, Holland, North Italy, Greece and Jugoslavia stories have been constantly coming in of German atrocities. It was the same in the Far East, the Japanese treatment of prisoners during transport being particularly outrageous. . . .'

My growing uneasiness was not allayed by the resignation early in January, 1945, from the Chair of the U.N. War Crimes Commission of Sir Cecil Hurst, the sound and experienced British judge on the Court of International Justice at the Hague. But I had to agree with my old friend the late Lord Tyrrell who shared my views on the matter: given the strength of American opinion, it would be premature to draw public attention to the dangers into which we were drifting.—Then the war came to an end. Immersed in my post-war occupation I lost sight of these issues until the publication of the Nuremberg Judgement caused me to put down a list of questions to which I could find no answer. Like the overture to a grand opera they give a hint of some of the leading themes of later Chapters of this book:—

Some Questions

" (1) Was it right or wise to decide that the Court for a trial of such tremendous importance to the future should be composed solely of judges nominated by those Members of the United Nations which had borne the brunt of the fighting, without any judge from less biased Member States or from more impartial neutral States ?

" Supposing, for example, that we had lost the war, as we nearly did, would we have been satisfied with a trial by Germans, Italians and Japanese, and would history have been expected to accept the results ?

[1] In this book the words ' politics ' and ' political ' has no reference to party politics.

" (2) **Is** it proposed that a similar trial should take place of *Allied* Governments (e.g. Russia) and individuals that *prima facie* have been guilty of planning, preparing, initiating and waging war of aggression against neighbouring countries, involving violation of the Kellogg-Briand Pact and other international treaties ; guilty also of ill-treatment and deportation to slave labour, or for other purposes, of civilian populations of or in occupied territory, plunder of private property, wanton destruction of cities, towns or villages, or devastation not justified by military necessity, and other crimes mentioned in the Charter ?

" (3) In the absence of such a trial (which is of course out of the question) does not the whole Nuremberg policy suggest that there is one law for victors and another for the vanquished ? *Vae victis* ! Is not that a bad precedent for the future ?

" (4) Was not political evidence an essential factor in the case for extenuation of the political charges ? Why, for example, is no mention made in the account of the background of the aggressive war of such provocations and humiliations as the occupation of the Ruhr in 1923, which was denounced as an aggression by every political party in Great Britain and in some Dominions; the employment of black troops in the Rhineland ; the intensive propaganda for the separation of the Rhineland and Bavaria ; the incessant demands for reparations in money and in kind, which were only dropped at Lausanne in 1932 ? Was it not these actions which, cumulatively, reduced the German people to utter exasperation, and in part led to their acceptance of Hitler and his gang, in spite of their abominations ? Was not such an accumulation of provocations tantamount to a major aggression ?

" Why, also, is there no mention of the failure of the League of Nations and the Allies to read the times aright ; to re-arm, and to stop the whole business before it was too late ? Was it not the failure to do so which encouraged Hitler, swelled his head, and led directly to these appalling events ? Is it not a perversion of history to set out the background of the judgement without this aspect ?

" (5) Is it not a fact that when the defendants tried to raise political issues of this kind, which appear to the layman as the obvious basis of their defence, they were ruled out of order ?

" (6) Was sufficient weight given to the overwhelming domination of Hitler, the almost supernatural popularity and personal ascendancy that he achieved; his dictatorial powers and insane intolerance of criticism or opposition ? Was not any-one opposing him liable, not as in constitutionally governed countries like our own merely to dismissal or resignation, but to incarceration in the dreaded internment camps (Schacht), or even to the fate of Röhm and many others, unless, like Hess and Papen, he could find a way of slipping out of the net in which he was caught ? In a war of survival, when it is difficult to keep a cool head, is not the consideration ' my country right or wrong ' important ?

" (7) Is not the fairness of the judgement on the political side vitiated by the omission of all these extenuating circumstances ? "

I discussed these questions with politicians, members of the fighting services, civil servants, lawyers, scientists, engineers and others, but received no reassuring answers. Many had misgivings about the effect of the Judgement on defensive preparations and on a future war. One stock comment was ' It is one more danger added to war '; and another was the inadequate one that no defendant had been condemned to death at the Nuremberg trial unless he had been found guilty of conventional war crimes.

Three months later the issue of such trials obtruded itself in an uglier form. For in Christmas week, 1946, Mr. George Furness, the indefatigable American counsel for Mr. Mamoru Shigemitsu, Japanese Ambassador in London before the out-break of war with Japan, arrived from Tokyo to collect evidence on behalf of his client. The news that so trusted a friend was to be tried as a war criminal came as a sharp blow because it had hitherto been understood that Shigemitsu's name was not on the list of persons to be tried. It now transpired that after the arrival of the Russian Judge his name had been added : Mr. Shigemitsu had been Japanese Ambassador to Moscow before coming to London.

There crowded into my mind a number of happy recollections of this fine representative of the Japanese diplomats of the old school. I recalled our first contact. Early in 1939 he had handed me a delightful letter of congratulations on my peerage

coming from two outstanding Japanese statesmen, Baron
Makino of the Paris Peace Conference (of 1919) and from
Mr. Yoshida who was to become Prime Minister of his country
in 1949. He added that ' they share with many of your friends
the renewed appreciation which is due to your distinguished
achievements in the cause of peace '—a typical touch from this
lifelong worker for peace. I recalled too the conversations
which the late Lord Lloyd and I myself, with the authority of
Lord Halifax and the knowledge of the Prime Minister,
Mr. Winston Churchill, had held with Mr. Shigemitsu and
others in the second half of 1940 in an endeavour to find
a way which would keep Japan out of the war. I remembered
how he had pressed for a British mission to go out to Japan and
that I was designated to head it.

Events had caught that plan up before it could be executed,
but I remembered how, after Lord Lloyd's death, Shigemitsu
had refused to relinquish his efforts. This had led to a four-
hour conversation with the Ambassador in March, 1941, at the
house in Surrey of Major-General Francis Piggott, former
Military Attaché at Tokyo, which resulted in my persuading the
Prime Minister to secure a priority air passage to Lisbon for
this crippled man with his wooden leg. Thence he was to battle
his way across Spain and France to Berne, there to meet his
Foreign Minister, Matsuoka in an effort to counter the blandish-
ments of Berlin and Rome, and maybe to persuade him to take
his homeward journey through Britain and America.

But unfortunately that plan was blocked too. I recalled the
impression Shigemitsu had made on all who met him, his outspoken patriotism, blended with the unconcealed conviction
that in case of war his country would start brilliantly and end
badly, his intense desire to report home correctly the views we
had expressed to justify our certainty that in the long run
Britain and America, the two great sea powers, must win.
Sometimes this desire was carried to the point of reading out
extracts from his draft despatches to make sure he had put the
matter correctly.

Yes. A big effort had to be made to save this man. He was
no criminal. So Christmas festivities went to the winds—but
not their fine spirit, I trust—while I immersed myself in files and
diaries and records.

In November, 1948, after twenty-two months of anxious waiting which had been punctuated by disturbing rumours about the Tokyo trials, the savage truth was out : seven had been sentenced to death by hanging ; sixteen to imprisonment for life ; Togo, an ex-Foreign Minister sentenced to imprisonment for twenty years ; and Shigemitsu, also an ex-Foreign Minister as well as an Ambassador, to seven years' imprisonment of which three years had already been thus spent while he had had to wait for this trial and judgement.

When that news reached here only a few days remained before the sentences were to be confirmed or reduced, there was no time to organize any large petition. But thanks to the indefatigable energy of Major-General Francis Piggott, who had received an urgent and informing telegram from Mr. Furness, an appeal for clemency was drawn up and telegraphed to General MacArthur. It had been signed by Mr. R. A. Butler, Sir Robert Craigie, Sir. Edward Crowe, Mr. Arthur Edwardes, Mr. H. A. Gwynne (the former editor of the *Morning Post*), myself, Sir Francis Lindley (formerly His Majesty's Ambassador in Tokyo) Major-General Francis Piggott and Lord Sempill.

This appeal for a revision of the judgement produced no effect whatsoever. So far as is known also, in spite of the fact that Shigemitsu's *bona fides* had been attested to by the ex-Prime Minister (Mr. Churchill), a former Minister without Portfolio in the War Cabinet (myself) with rather unique experience in international affairs, an ex-Parliamentary Secretary in the Foreign Office (Mr. R. A. Butler), three British ex-Ambassadors, two of them with experience at Tokyo, and an equally large number of distinguished Americans, His Majesty's Government never moved a finger to aid this old friend of Great Britain; as recently as May 19, 1949, they flatly declined to do so. Neither did the administration in Washington intervene.

On returning in March, 1949, from an unavoidable absence of nearly three months in Egypt on important Suez Canal business, I found among the huge accumulations of correspondence a mass of material from Japan. Its perusal revealed, in an exaggerated degree, many of the features of the Nuremberg trials that had led me to formulate the list of probing questions at the head of this Introduction. In addition.

there were perturbing features that were peculiar to the Tokyo trials. No one, I thought, with a spark of conscience could leave the matter where it lay. But it was not easy to decide what to do, especially as the records of the Tokyo trials proved to be almost incredibly cumbrous, and only one copy was available. It was in the Foreign Office library.

Then there caught my eye on the order paper of the House of Lords a motion by the Bishop of Chichester calling attention to the present situation in regard to war crimes trials in Germany. With the Bishop's prompt approval a similar motion was put down, substituting 'Japan' for Germany, with a suggestion that the two motions should be taken on the same day. The Foreign Office in the House of Lords, however, thought that this was rather too large a subject for a single session. So I had to be content with a separate day exactly a fortnight later.

This arrangement made it possible for me to support the Bishop of Chichester's motion on May 5, 1949, by launching a major attack on the origin, principles and policy of these Trials, the immorality of their conception during the war in an atmosphere of mutual hate, their effect in lengthening the war and blocking the way to an earlier peace, and rendering a peace treaty impossible to achieve. I was also enabled to follow it up on May 19, by exposing some of the weaknesses of the Tokyo trials as illustrated particularly by the case of Shigemitsu. Never again must such things be, and there was no use in hushing up what was being whispered everywhere one went.

The debates, however, proved rather unsatisfactory. They started too late in the day, were interrupted, overlapped one into the other and many arguments and counter-arguments on either side remained unanswered. The press and other organs of publicity did not report them fully, if at all, another consequence, no doubt, of the lateness of the hour at which the matter could be raised.

In these circumstances a request from Pen-in-Hand to write this book was very welcome.

Acknowledgements are made for the great assistance received from Major-General Francis Piggott, Captain Russell Grenfell, R.N., Mr. George Furness, his colleague Mr. Ben Bruce Blakeney, Chairman of the Defence Counsel at the Tokyo trials, and Mr. F. W. Pick, whose *Contemporary History* has revealed information of great importance that had hitherto escaped my attention but bears on some of these problems of Politics, Trials and Errors. I am indebted also for inspiration and suggestion to *Advance to Barbarism* by F. J. P. Veale, who wrote as ' A Jurist '; it displays great knowledge of the military art and profound research into the historical aspects of all that relates to War Crimes Trials.

Two remarkable new books published in America, Mr. Montgomery Belgion's *Victors' Justice* and Freda Utley's *The High Cost of Vengeance*, appear to take the same general line as I do and both contain a vast amount of information about the subsidiary trials in Germany, which is often of a very disturbing character. As, however, the policy of Great Britain and America on those trials appears now to be on sound lines and as information on the subject of the subsidiary trials both in Germany and Japan is rather scanty I have not penetrated far into that subject. My book is limited rather to the political aspects and results of war crimes trials, unconditional surrender, aggression as left by the Nuremberg and Tokyo trials and corrected by the United Nations Declaration on Human Rights, December, 1948, and kindred matters.

CHAPTER ONE

TRIALS AND AGGRESSION

War Crimes in World War I

' GEORGE ! If you take my advice you will not touch it ! If you do, believe me, you will always regret it ! '

As I burst into the Prime Minister's room to report for duty after a bout of influenza contracted during the Paris armistice negotiations, I caught those words addressed in an Elder Statesman's bantering tones to Mr. Lloyd George who was rather cross. Cross, firstly because he disliked being addressed as ' George ', and secondly because he did not want to be chaffed out of the idea of the trial of the Kaiser before he had made up his mind about it. This notion had cropped up at a conversation between Lord Curzon and M. Clemenceau in Paris and was to come before the Imperial War Cabinet next day, November 20, 1918. But it was shrewd advice, which, had it been followed, would have saved the Leaders of the Allied and Associated Powers a lot of difficulties and prevented some loss of prestige. That was the first time I ever heard of War Crimes Trials.

On the following day I was present again when the matter was raised officially for the first time at the Imperial War Cabinet. It received a mixed reception. The cooler heads were distinctly chary; but eventually the question was referred to the Law Officers of the Crown who, as might be expected, seized on it with alacrity.[1]

It came up again on November 28, when Sir F. E. Smith, the Attorney-General (afterwards Lord Birkenhead) carried the whole of the Imperial War Cabinet off their feet with a statement of extraordinary power and eloquence. The trial of the Kaiser before a legal tribunal was approved so far as the nations of the British Empire were concerned[2]—although, as we shall see, there were still some doubters.

[1] David Lloyd George, *The Truth About the Peace Treaties*, pp. 94–100.
[2] *Ibid*, pp. 100–114.

In my usual rôle of Secretary I was functioning once more a few days later, on December 2, when Mr. Lloyd George brought the proposal, which included the Attorney-General's opinion, before a meeting of the Allies—M. Clemenceau, Signor Orlando and Baron Sonnino ; owing to Colonel House's illness there was no representative of the U.S.A. The only out and out opponent of the proposal was the Italian Foreign Minister, that sturdy, obstinate, likeable, half-Italian, half-Welsh statesman Baron Sonnino, who made a number of telling points : Did they want to make the Kaiser a martyr ? Was not the *Bundesrath* just as responsible ? Could the responsibility be fastened on to the leaders of a nation either for the war itself or for war crimes ? Was not the nation itself really responsible ? Had not Napoleon's banishment to St. Helena benefited the Bonapartists and brought back the régime of the would-be dictator Napoleon III ?

But the Premier, Signor Orlando, for once, did not back up his Foreign Minister. And no one else opposed the trial. Even Mr. Bonar Law, one of the cool heads, had to agree that this proposal to try the Kaiser would be popular and it was adopted in principle, subject to President Wilson's agreement. On details, however, the proposal did not have so smooth a passage. Signor Orlando considered that the constitution of the Court presented almost insurmountable difficulties. Baron Sonnino asked what would be done if the Dutch refused to give the Kaiser up: he did not get a very convincing answer, and history was to vindicate his doubts. Mr. Balfour, while not opposing the proposal as such, brought out the difficulties prophetically: if the trial was to be fair, and to convince the world that it was fair, neutrals would presumably have to be included in the Tribunal. All sorts of political issues would then be raised. The Allies would lay themselves open to all the delays of the law, which would weary the whole world. Like the trial of Warren Hastings it might last seven years. If, as M. Clemenceau had suggested, the Court was to be composed only of Allied judges, would not this take away all appearance of impartiality ? ' If the Allies set up the Court themselves what would be the moral effect upon the world ? ' [1]

---

[1] David Lloyd George, *The Truth About the Peace Treaties*, pp. 137 141.

There spoke another of the cool heads. What Mr. Balfour said in 1918 half the world was saying in 1948 about yet another set of political trials ! But the hot heads brushed his arguments aside. The proposal was cabled that very day to Washington; and President Wilson, according to Mr. Lloyd George, eventually agreed. For long after, on our many Channel crossings, Mr. Lloyd George was wont to gaze at the solid mass of Dover Castle perched on the white cliffs of old England and to murmur—' That's the place for the Kaiser's trial! '

It is not without interest to recall that on December 4, Sir Robert Borden, the Prime Minister of Canada, another of the cool heads, summoned me at an early hour to protest strongly against the decision of the Allies to try the Kaiser, and especially against the despatch of Mr. Lloyd George's telegram to President Wilson. His objection was made on the ground that there had been an understanding that the question should not be decided without further discussion at the Imperial War Cabinet. He was never enthusiastic about these trials.

The following telegram to President Wilson sent by Colonel House from his sick-bed in Paris likewise deserves notice : ' December 5, 1918. Clemenceau called in the afternoon to tell me of the London meeting. We talked of that part of the resolution related to the trial of the Kaiser. He is in favour of it in a mild way. Sonnino last night expressed himself against it. He thought it would merely create sympathy and would do no good. He thought Holland would refuse to give him up and we would be imprudent to make her '.[1]

Enough has been said to show that in 1918 the drive in this matter came mainly from Great Britain. Up to this point the worst with which the defeated enemy had been threatened was 'international outlawry'. Mr. Lloyd George and his colleagues had not as yet mentioned the subject in public. With its inclusion, however, in the General Election manifesto of all three Parties, public opinion was worked up to a high pitch. The expression ' hanging the Kaiser ' became the most popular catch-phrase of the day. Soon the whole issue got out of hand.

The subject next came on to the Agenda paper of the Paris Peace Conference, which set up for its consideration an

[1] *The Intimate Papers of Colonel House*, Vol. IV, p. 251.

important Commission which, with its three sub-Committees, embraced such an aggregation of international legal talent as can rarely have assembled for so futile a task.[1]

Gradually, however, the extravagant ideas that had pervaded the earlier discussions were whittled away. On March 12, 1919, Mr. Lansing, American Secretary of State and Chairman of the Commission, told the Council of Ten that his Commission ' had not attempted to draw up a list of war criminals because the Sub-Committee, dealing with the responsibility for the war, had decided that no one could be tried under that particular head. That is to say, the Sub-Committee had come to the conclusion that the accused could not be brought before any legal tribunal, since they were only guilty of a moral responsibility '.[2]

This was a shock to the Statesmen of the Five Principal Powers. By that time it was impossible for them to go back —just as it was for their successors in 1945. On April 16, President Wilson had still thought that the Kaiser might be tried ' for a high misdemeanour, which might not legally (sic) amount to a crime '. And the South African Premier, Botha, had insisted on going on record that at least the people to be tried must be named. Would you undertake to give up men for trial without being told their names, he had asked Kitchener, in 1902. ' As a soldier ', Kitchener had replied he would not.[3]

The Allied Leaders had had the wisdom to avoid the subject during the war; but afterwards public opinion had been whipped up at the British post-war General Election and elsewhere and they had become irrevocably committed. So the Treaty of Versailles had to provide for the public arraignment of the Kaiser for a supreme offence against international morality and the sanctity of Treaties (Articles 227–228) and his trial by a special Tribunal of five judges, appointed by the Principal Allied and Associated Powers. There was to be an American, British, French, Italian, and Japanese judge.

---

[1] *Foreign Relations of the United States. The Paris Peace Conference*, 1919. Vol. III, pp. 63–5, gives the Directory.

[2] *Ibid*, Vol. IV, pp. 332–3. The Author's presence at this meeting is recorded.

[3] *Ibid.*, Vol. IV, p. 482, and Vol. V, p. 471.

Persons accused of violation of the laws and customs of war were to be brought before military Tribunals of the Victors.

The real difficulties, however, were only about to begin ! The Kaiser had crossed into Holland on November 10, 1918. The Netherland's Government very soon let it be known that they attached great importance to the right of asylum and would not give him up. They had the courage to stick to their principles. It was not until January 16, 1920, that the Peace Conference sent a pompous letter demanding the handing over of the Kaiser and mentioning among the crimes for which he was responsible a list nearly as long as the Nuremberg indictment after the second World War, *e.g.*—cynical violation of the neutrality of Belgium and Luxemburg ; the barbarous and pitiless system of hostages ; mass deportations ; carrying off of young girls from Lille who were delivered up to the worst atrocities ; systematic devastation of territories without military objects ; unrestricted submarine warfare including abandonment of victims on the high seas, and innumerable acts against non-combatants.

Nearly all these acts were crimes and certainly horrible. They deserved punishment. But could anything be more absurd than to lay them all at the door of the Kaiser ? At any rate, the Dutch Government in its reply on January 23, 1920, called the bluff of the Allies. After remaining neutral all through the war, it refused to admit that ' it was an international duty to associate itself with the act of high international policy of the Allied Powers '. If, on the other hand, an international jurisdiction were established for such purposes, Holland would be there.[1] By this firm policy the Netherlands Government probably saved the Allies an infinity of difficulties and the risks foreseen by Baron Sonnino and Mr. Balfour. Many people besides the Kaiser himself breathed more freely.

And as to the War Criminals, in spite of the decision of Mr. Lansing's Commission, a list of the chief persons to be tried was at last published at the end of January, 1920. It included well-known people such as the Crown Prince of Germany, Prince Rupprecht of Bavaria, F.M. von Mackensen, General von Kluck, Admiral von Tirpitz and Admiral von Capelle.

[1] *The Annual Register*, 1920, p. 254.

But during the year it was decided that, as the Kaiser was not available for trial, it would be difficult to press forward vigorously with the punishment of those who, however important, had only been the Emperor's servants.

So the famous trials by the Allies never took place after all. The Germans were asked to do the job instead (as in 1949). But at the Spa Conference later in the year (July, 1920) it transpired that they had been extremely dilatory. Efforts to ' ginger them up ' were not very successful. Nine trials took place before the German Supreme Court between May 23, 1921, and the end of the year. There were several acquittals and a few of the trials were followed by imprisonment in a fortress. But public opinion was by then as sick of the trials as it is to-day, after the Second World War. They faded out of sight and mind. As Lord Winster put it in the House of Lords' debate on May 19, 1949 : ' As a race we are not good haters, and we have an engrained partiality for " calling it a day " when the contest is over '.

The fiasco of these trials, it may be said, contributed to the desire for a change of Government that was growing up all over the country in 1922. It certainly vindicated the Elder Statesman's warning quoted at the head of this Chapter. Yet its main historical value is in its warning to future Governments: did they learn the lesson ?

War Crimes in World War II

Although the subject of war crimes had often been mentioned in parliament and press, the first formal reference to a War Crimes Policy in World War II was made in a speech by Mr. Winston Churchill when dealing with Unconditional Surrender in the House of Commons on February 11, 1943. He there said that ' *justice must be done upon the wicked and the guilty.* . . .' The second time the world heard of it was two days later (February 13) in a broadcast by President Roosevelt. Again it occurred in a passage on Unconditional Surrender. He said: ' we do mean to impose punishment upon the guilty barbaric leaders '. In the minds and in the speeches of both the great leaders of the Western countries, therefore, the idea of War Crimes Tribunals grew up as part and parcel of their policy of unconditional surrender.

After that the subject lay more or less dormant until the Moscow Conference of October, 1943, when the Foreign Ministers of the United States of America, the United Kingdom, and the Soviet Union—U.S.A., U.K., and U.S.S.R., the three U's—issued (on November 1) on behalf of President Roosevelt, Mr. Churchill, and Marshal Stalin a manifesto stating that Germans implicated in atrocities in the countries overrun would be taken to the countries in which their crimes were committed and charged and punished according to those countries' Laws. That decision, it was stated, did not prejudice the case of the major war criminals, and of those whose offences had no particular geographical location ; these would be punished by a joint decision of the Allies.

Beyond the appointment in October, 1943, of the United Nations War Crimes Commission in London under the Chairmanship of Sir Cecil Hurst (who resigned in 1945) to draw up a list of war criminals, little consideration was given by any of the Allied Governments to the question of procedure until the Crimea Conference at Yalta when the President, the Prime Minister and Marshal Stalin announced their ' inflexible purpose ' *inter alia* to ' bring all war criminals to just and swift punishment '.[1] From a ' Protocol ' of the Proceedings, which was not published until 1947 (Cmd. 7088), it seems that the question of the *major war criminals* was to have been the subject of enquiry by the three Foreign Secretaries for report, in due course, after the close of the Conference. That Report, if it was ever completed, does not seem to have been published, and for a long time there was a black-out on public information about what was happening behind the scenes. It was lifted only in February, 1949, when the American State Department released for publication a book on the International Conference on Military Trials, held in London in 1945.[2] This throws a flood of light on the subject.

It is of great interest that on April 23, 1945, Sir Alexander Cadogan handed to Judge Samuel Rosenman, assistant to the American President, an *aide-mémoire* outlining the views of His Majesty's Government on the difficulties of a trial of war criminals. It was rather in the vein of the opponents to the

[1] Report of the Crimea Conference, February 11, 1945, Cmd. 6598.
[2] United States Department of State. Publication 3080.

trial of the Kaiser in 1919—and favoured a political decision, not a legal process.

Sir Alexander Cadogan stated that Hitler and other arch-criminals ought to suffer the penalty of death for their crimes, but he rather inclined towards a political decision by the Allies, as had also been discussed in 1918. He pointed out that a trial of the pre-war conduct of the Nazi leaders and of their crimes during the war would be exceedingly long and elaborate. Even so people would say that it was a ' put-up job ' designed by the Allies to justify a punishment already resolved on—all this was rather reminiscent of Mr. Balfour's attitude in 1918. If the trials dragged on, our Permanent Under Secretary of State feared that public opinion would weary of them. Eventually the trials might even be denounced as a farce ! The charges would have to include Hitler's conduct before the war and his unprovoked attacks since the declarations of war on various countries. ' *These are not war crimes in the ordinary sense, nor is it at all clear they can properly be described as crimes under international law.*'[1] He also hinted at the risks we would run by declaring as crimes against international law actions which had not been treated as such in the past. This too recalls the attitude of Mr. Lansing's Commission at the Peace Conference of 1919.

That prescient *aide-mémoire*, however, which came as a breath of fresh air into an over-heated situation, was not at all to the liking of the United States, who had been at work for some time on an elaborate plan for judicial trials. And a few weeks later, Britain toed the line, and a fresh *aide-mémoire* dated June 3, 1945, was sent to Washington which ' accepted in principle the U.S. draft as a basis for discussion '.[2]

Second thoughts are not always the best. Now we were committed irrevocably to a draft which—with the addition of some British amendments—was submitted by the American State Department to the Foreign Ministers of France, Great Britain, and the Soviet Union at the San Francisco Conference. On June 26 the four nations met in Conference in London to consider the draft in detail, and on August 8, 1945, the Agree-

[1] Author's italics.

[2] United States Department of State. Publication 3080, pp. 18 and 41. To the surprise of Mr. Henry Stimson ' the principal opposition to legal proceedings came from the British . . . but with French and Russian support the American view prevailed '. (*On Active Service in Peace and War*. Henry L. Stimson and Mr. McGeorge Bundy.)

ment covering the Charter of the Nuremberg Trials was published. (Cmd. 6668.)

In view of the great and fundamental differences that revealed themselves at this Conference, it is remarkable that agreement should ever have been reached at all. To begin with, the judicial concepts of some of the Powers concerned were found to be totally different. Those of Britain and America were, of course, similar in principle, though subject to variations in procedure. But the French system was based on the Roman Law of Western Europe, while the Russian system derived from the Roman idea, which had however reached her chiefly from the Eastern Empire via Byzantium. One of the fundamental differences for example arose from the fact that ' *the Soviet views a Court as one of the organs of government power, a weapon in the hands of the ruling class for the purpose of safeguarding its interests* ', whereas the British and American systems treat ' *a Court as an independent agency responsible only before the law* '[1].

The distinguished authorities who achieved agreement on those conflicting bases must be congratulated on the accomplishment of a very remarkable feat ; but the same ' stubborn and deep discords ' as they had encountered were bound to crop up at the trials, to the detriment of justice. One can see them at work in the dissenting opinion of the Russian judge at the Nuremberg Trial who opposed every decision of the majority which took into account mitigating circumstances. That same spirit—savouring revenge—must have actuated the Russian judge in his approach to every decision. We can see it at work again and again at the Tokyo trials. Is it to that cause that we must attribute the severity of the sentences at both Nuremberg and Tokyo ?

This contradictory attitude lends tremendous support to the growing number of people who hold that the mere fact of the existence of such fundamental differences of principle makes it impossible for international courts of law to provide an adequate standard of justice, especially in a trial of human beings for their lives. Even if, *per impossibile,* justice were achieved, it cannot inspire public confidence at home or abroad, neither in the present nor in the future.

[1] Author's italics. A similar statement in A. Vishinsky's work on Soviet law, *The Law of the Soviet State.*

Aggression

Although the London Conference of June, 1945, patched up many of the differences there were others where it failed, notably in the question of a definition of aggression for which the Americans were pressing. That large subject requires careful examination. If the United States Delegates failed to obtain agreement on a definition—this is not surprising, for the subject has troubled mankind since the dawn of history.

An Ancient Precedent

Thucydides can always be relied on for precedents, and an interesting case occurs in his story of the origins of the Peloponnesian War. In the two Conferences of the Lacedaemonian peoples before the outbreak of war in 431 B.C., it was constantly urged that a decent pretext must be found to justify war against an Athens, whose increasing power was viewed with alarm. The most attractive suggestion was Corinth's claim that Athens had broken a Treaty in besieging Potidaea, a town on the Gulf of Salonica. After obtaining the confirmation of the Delphic Oracle, the highest spiritual authority in a religious, not to say superstitious community, the Conference formally denounced the siege as an act of aggression in breach of treaty and adjourned to prepare for war in a year's time. In order to ensure their moral position before declaring war, however, they sent Ambassadors to Athens and charged them with a number of complaints and with instructions to find as good a pretext for war as possible. The siege of Potidaea, however, seems to have held the field. But Thucydides lets the truth out by admitting that the Lacedaemonians ' feared the growth of the power of the Athenians, seeing most of Hellas already subject to them '.[1]

This is the prototype of the story of aggression down the ages : the fear that some rival nation is becoming too powerful (the *cause* of the war) ; the idea of ' collective ' security ; a preventive war ; the moral doubts that make it necessary, for the sake of public opinion, to find a plausible *pretext* for the war—to put the blame on the other fellow if possible ! In Chapter IV on the Norway affair we shall find Hitler and our-

[1] Thucydides. *The Peloponnesian War*, Book I, Ch. III and V.

selves, however different our starting-points and aims, both hesitating to put our respective plans into operation—vitally important as both of them were—until a pretext could be found; and in the end we both had to start, almost simultaneously, without having either of us made out a cast-iron case !

Perhaps the episode of Potidaea and other examples in Thucydides prompted Polybius, a rather neglected historian,[1] to insist more than once on the importance of the ' distinction between a pretext and a cause, or again between a cause and a beginning of a war '.[2] But appreciation of the importance of a pretext was not confined to the Greeks. Polybius also records that ' the Romans were wont to take care *not to appear to be the aggressors*,[3] or to attack their neighbours without provocation ; but to be considered always to be acting in self-defence, and only to enter upon war under compulsion '.[4] Examples of that are to be found in Livy and other Roman writers. It is important to keep in mind the distinction between cause and pretext even in modern times, as we shall see later in this chapter. It tends to check hasty conclusions as to who is the real aggressor.

The long story of aggression down the ages may be read in history books. A glance at the record of some of the belligerent countries, however, is called for in this context. How else can we judge our own Trials and Errors ?

The Enemy's Record

There is no doubt that in the light of history all our enemies have an evil record as aggressors. Frederick the Great's occupation of Silesia in 1740 without declaration of war was described by H. A. L. Fisher ' as an act of the blackest treachery '. The three partitions of Poland towards the end of the eighteenth century in which Austria and Russia shared, were equally black—especially as Germany and Austria had guaranteed

---

[1] Lord Chatham's instructions for the education at Oxford of his son. William Pitt included the advice to read Thucydides and Polybius.

[2] The *Histories of Polybius*, e.g. Book XXII, ch. 8.

[3] Author's italics.

[4] The *Histories of Polybius*, shorter fragments.

Poland. Just as heinous was the Austro-German attack on Denmark on February 1, 1864, when Bismarck deluded the Danish Government into believing a false report that England had threatened Prussia with intervention in the event of hostilities. No less sordid was Bismarck's publication in a mutilated form of his Emperor's famous telegram from Ems, the alteration in emphasis of which precipitated a declaration of war by France and appeared to place on her the onus of aggression. No pretence of a pretext, however was presented in the case of the flagrant German aggression against Belgium in August, 1914. Hitler, of course never dreamt of even looking for an excuse when he attacked Poland in September, 1939.

Modern Italy also has a bad reputation for aggression as instanced by the attack on Tripoli (North Africa) in 1911 with hardly a shadow of a pretext, d'Annunzio's *coup-de-main* at Fiume in 1919, Mussolini's seizure of Corfu in 1923 and invasion of Abyssinia in 1935, and the occupation of Albania in March, 1939.

In the case of Japan also the list of aggressions in modern times is serious—the sinking of the Chinese transport Kowshing in 1894 without declaration of war, which ushered in the Sino-Japanese war of 1894 ; the torpedo-boat attack on the Russian fleet at Port Arthur in February, 1904, which opened the Russo-Japanese war, and before its declaration, the invasion of Manchuria in September, 1931, and the sudden attack on the American fleet in Pearl Harbour on December 7, 1941.

The danger of aggression even before World War I was so fully realized that, as the result of an inquiry by the Committee of Imperial Defence under Mr. Asquith's personal direction in 1908, which included the historical aspects, a ' bolt from the blue '—an attack in time of profound peace—was adopted as one of the basic assumptions of our defensive preparations.

The black records of the enemy Powers, however, would not justify the assumption that their aggressions in World War II or in earlier wars were all made without provocation, or that no acts of aggression had been perpetrated by the Allies. This, clearly, must be substantiated. Let us take the Allies in turn and first consider Russia.

The Soviet Record

Modern Russia is so different in many ways from the old Empire that some might think it perhaps hardly worth our while to examine in detail the historical aggressions of the Tsars. As already mentioned, however, Russia shared Germany's and Austria's guilt in the eighteenth-century partitions of Poland.

In World War II, however, the Soviet's record in the matter of aggressions in breach of Treaty is well nigh scandalous. Non-aggression pacts were entered into by the Soviet Union with Estonia and Latvia in 1932, with Finland and Lithuania in 1926, with Poland on January 26, 1934. It is ironical that Stalin's Foreign Minister proposed a Definition of Aggression and embodied it in a Convention which was signed in 1933 by all the European neighbours of the Soviet Union and Russia. This together with all the other treaties was broken during 1939 long before Germany attacked Russia. And the forcible establishment during the war and the maintenance after the war and to this very day of Soviet hegemony over the nations behind the Iron Curtain—not to mention downright annexation—is equally repellent. The record is given in greater detail in Chapter Eight.

The Polish Record

Another ally, Poland, who has been the victim of innumerable aggressions herself, is unfortunately not blameless in this matter. Between the two wars there occurred two Polish aggressions. The first was General Zeligowski's seizure of Vilna, the capital of Lithuania, an act finally accepted by the Great Powers in 1923. The second was the annexation in 1938, when her neighbour Czechoslovakia was in dire distress, of a ' Naboth's vineyard ' in Teschen, eventually amounting (including some territory ceded early in 1939) to 1,000 square miles, with 228,000 inhabitants of whom 133,000 were Czechs.

The French Record

France also cannot claim exemption from the charge of having committed acts of aggression in modern times. If we do not think of Napoleon I, some of Napoleon III's ventures, in Italy in 1859 for example, and in Mexico, come very near aggression, although in the Italian case he took care to insist that Cavour should provide him with a pretext. Also the occupation of the Ruhr in 1923 was held in Great Britain to have been illegal and a breach of the Treaty of Versailles, though the French Government always contested this view.

The British Record

We are perhaps rather apt to feel superior about ' aggression ' but, in fact, are not as innocent as all that. Without going back so far as the Elizabethan adventurers there comes to mind Nelson's sinking of the Danish fleet at Copenhagen in April, 1804, and the bombardment of the forts. Nelson, who was acting under the orders of his Government was undoubtedly right from a strategical point of view; if, however, he had been captured by his enemies and tried under the provisions of say the Nuremberg or Tokyo Charters, would he not have been hanged as a ' war criminal ' ? We shall probably be told that times have changed since then: if so, it might seem to some that human nature has not changed for the better since the days of Thucydides.

The speculation is not quite so academic as it sounds. Indeed, it is highly topical. Since the appearance of the Second Volume of Mr. Churchill's *Second World War* there has been sharp criticism in France about the late Admiral of the Fleet Sir James Somerville's Bombardment of the French fleet at Mers-el-Kebir (Oran) on July 3, 1940. In a series of three brilliant articles on the subject[1] M. Pierre Varillon, has even compared that deplorable episode to Nelson's action at Copenhagen.[2] Although to my personal knowledge, feeling on this subject is strong among many French naval officers who are good friends of this country, this is not the occasion to describe the operation which involved the death of 1,300 French seamen and the loss of valuable French warships. It was deeply deplored by every one on either side who had any concern in it. One is entitled, however, to speculate whether, had we lost the war (which was very much in the balance at that time) and a Nazi Court had been set up on Nuremberg principles,

[1] *La Revue des Deux Mondes*, May 1, May 15, and June 1, 1949.
[2] Also mentioned by W. Churchill, *The Second World War*, Vol. II, p. 206.

Mr. Churchill, the Board of Admiralty, the Naval Commanders-in-Chief—and even minor Ministers of Cabinet rank like myself who knew nothing of the matter until they read it in the press—would not have been charged, as Shigemitsu was charged, with the crime of ' waging aggressive warfare ' and have received heavy sentences. And this on the assumption that the enemy had used our own code of conduct ! The fact that Sir James Somerville, one of the finest seamen and characters I ever knew, objected,[1] and that the Admiralty also deplored the decision of the War Cabinet, would hardly have saved them from the inexorable provisions of Art. 8 of the Charter, *viz.* ' The fact that the Defendant acted pursuant to order of his Government or of a superior shall not free him from responsibility, but may be considered in mitigation of punishment if the Tribunal determines that justice so requires '.

This is a case where, in all probability, every past and present member of the Naval Service and the great mass of our fellow countrymen are convinced that the Board of Admiralty and Admiral Somerville were in duty bound to carry out the orders of the War Cabinet. Yet, on the Nuremberg and Tokyo precedents, it would seem that, had either the members of the Board or the Commander-in-Chief been put on trial, the best for which they could have hoped under the Charter would have been a possible mitigation of punishment.

We have to put into the same category as Mers-el-Kebir the three days' bombardment by British and Free French (de Gaullist) forces of Dakar towards the end of September, 1940, which resulted in severe damage to the modern French battleship *Richelieu* and the old British battleship *Resolution*, as well as some injury to two destroyers and the sinking of two Vichy submarines. This was unquestionably a technical aggression ; again at a German trial on Nuremberg or Tokyo lines, everyone concerned would probably have received severe sentences.

In these instances it must be remembered that we were not fighting Germans or Italians with whom we were at war, but

[1] Mr. Churchill's account says : ' The distress of the British Admiral and his principal officers was evident to us from the signals which passed. Nothing but the most direct orders compelled them to open fire on those who had been lately their comrades. At the Admiralty also there was manifest emotion ' (*The Second World War*, Vol. II, p. 209).

Frenchmen who had been waging war on Germany alongside of and in the same squadrons as our own seamen up to a week or two before the action at Mers-el-Kebir, and with whom we were not at war, though the Vichy Government was believed to be to a great extent dominated by our enemies.

Other operations by the Western Allies which would probably have been treated as aggressions by a Nazi Tribunal conducted on Nuremberg lines were the mining of the Norwegian Leads in April, 1940 (see Chapter IV); the landing early in 1941 of British troops in Iceland and their relief later in the year, but before U.S.A. had become a belligerent by American forces; in 1941 also the landing of British garrisons in the Azores, the Canaries and Cape Verde Islands; in 1942 the Anglo-American landings in Morocco, and Algeria, and the temporary invasion of Madagascar.

This partial and incomplete sketch is sufficient to show that for centuries past and in recent times, certainly during the war, technical aggressions have been committed by most of the principal allied European Powers. The Western Powers did not hesitate to ally themselves with an Eastern Power whose aggressions had been flagrant, recent and on a large scale. In spite of that the German political and military Leaders were singled out to be put on trial for their own aggressions and were not even allowed to make the point in their defence that their enemies had been doing the same thing right up to the date of the trial ' as evidence of a general practice accepted by Law ' (Art. 38, 1 (b) of the Statute of the International Court of Justice). Moreover, they were tried on a crime created by an *ex post facto* law drafted by the Victors for this particular Trial of the Vanquished. Yet, the Germans, and we ourselves, and all posterity are expected to accept that as a fair trial.

Disagreement on Definition
The London Conference, June, 1945

Against this background of ancient and modern history we must now examine the discussions on aggression of the London Conference of June–July, 1945,[1] which was appointed by the

---

[1] For the remainder of this Chapter the page references in brackets are to the American State Department's book, *International Conference on Military Trials*, London, 1945, unless otherwise stated.

Allied Governments " to make arrangements for preparing and prosecuting the charges, on the subject of aggression.[1]" Among other things they submitted an agreed draft of suggestions on procedure to assist the judges in preparing the rules. The leading figures at this ' informal ' Conference (for so it is described in the American report) were: for the United States, Mr. Robert Jackson, Associate Justice of the United States Supreme Court; for the United Kingdom, Sir David Maxwell Fyfe, Attorney-General until the change of Government towards the end of the Conference; for France, Professor Gros[2]; and for the Soviet Union, General Nikitchenko. The American and British representatives were both already designated as Prosecutors and the Russian delegate was destined to become one of the Judges at Nuremberg. The documents, and particularly the excellent shorthand notes, which, however, were not submitted to the British, French or Soviet Delegates, for verification and editing, illuminate the whole subject of the recent series of War Crimes Trials.

The task of the Conference was to ' bring all war criminals to just and swift punishment ' as decided by the Crimea (Yalta) Conference. They had therefore to *punish*, as the Russian Delegate never let them forget ; to be swift, or the world would get sick of the whole business and would start to gibe—as has happened since ; and to be fair, or it would be said—as it is being said to-day—that it was a trial by the Victors of the Vanquished, and a staged affair. They were, therefore, up against all the difficulties that had been foreseen before the Paris Peace Conference of 1919, and more recently in Sir Alexander Cadogan's *aide-mémoire*. Both the experience of last time, and the advice of Sir Alexander Cadogan were brushed aside.

It appears from the record that the United States were anxious to demonstrate by these trials that the war had from the outset been one of almost uniquely flagrant aggression by Nazi Germany which had been the justification of President Roosevelt's Lease-Lend scheme and of his whole policy towards the war. But, as we have seen, the Paris Peace Conference had been very hesitant about declaring aggression to be a criminal act in law and similar doubts had been expressed in the Cadogan

---

[1] *Hansard*, Commons, May 17, 1945, col. 2624.
[2] An alternate member to M. Falco.

aide-mémoire of April 23, 1945. However, none of the Delegates boggled much about declaring it to be, in the legal sense, a crime—which astonishes the lay mind. Very soon it was realized that the defendants would be likely to raise the question of what constituted an aggression. Unless the Charter contained something to prevent it, the defence would raise all the great international issues that had so gravely beset the inter-war period to explain their actions. That was the main reason for the American desire for a definition of aggression.

A few extracts from speeches made during the Conference will show its trend of thought :—

June 29. Sir David Maxwell Fyfe explained that the defendants might be compelled to put in writing the purposes for which evidence was going to be called ' in order to prevent mere political speeches being put in under the guise of evidence'; he continued: ' Otherwise a witness may suddenly be called into the box; we do not know what he is going to say, and he starts making political speeches in defence of German activities '. (pp. 100–101.)

On the legality of this disposition I am not entitled to an opinion, but to the layman, it seems very odd that two of the legal authorities, who had already been designated as Prosecutors at the trials, and a third, who was destined to become one of the judges, should have been selected to draw up the Charter of the very Court where they were to function. Without any reflection on the manner in which these distinguished jurists discharged their most difficult and delicate task this arrangement seems to offer opportunities to arrange the procedure to suit the Prosecution rather than the Defence! Could this happen except in the case of a Victors' Trial ?

To return to the Conference. Extracts from the remarks of Mr. Justice Jackson run as follows :—

June 29. *Mr. Justice Jackson* was discussing a proposal to forbid attempts to introduce irrelevant propaganda into speeches for the defence : ' If an offer of proof is irrelevant, it should be excluded merely because it is irrelevant. If it is relevant to the defence would it be conceivable to exclude it because it might have unpleasant political implications ? I suspect that critics will point at this phrase as indicating that there is something in our own positions that we are fearful of having exposed, if, even though it is relevant, we are proposing to exclude lines of inquiry which would be inconvenient for ourselves politically. . . .' (p. 102).

Mr. Justice Jackson it will be noticed throughout, was very conscious of the political risks of these trials. To continue:—

July 19. In the course of an explanation of an American definition of aggression *Mr. Justice Jackson* said : ' The point is that we take the actual attack, actual invasion, as constituting the aggression, and we cut off arguments that there wasn't an " attack " because invasion really was in defence against political or economic measures. Now Germany will undoubtedly contend, if we don't put this in, that this wasn't a war of aggression although it looked like it. They will say that in reality they were defending against encirclement or other remote menaces. Then you are in the whole political argument of who was doing what to whom in Europe before 1939.' (p. 302).

Again, it seems odd to a layman that the question should be raised by prospective prosecutors and judge to deprive the defendant's of their only line of defence and probably the only way of saving their lives. And yet the Governments involved indignantly deny that it was a trial of the Vanquished by the Victors! Is it conceivable that anything of the kind could have been allowed in the case of a neutral Court ?

The point is further emphasized in another passage at the same meeting :—

Mr. Justice Jackson. ' I really think that this trial, if it should get into an argument over the political and economic causes of this war, could do infinite harm, both in Europe, which I don't know well, and in America, which I know fairly well. If we should have a prolonged controversy over whether Germany invaded Norway a few jumps ahead of a British invasion of Norway, or whether France in declaring war was the real aggressor, this trial can do infinite harm for those countries with the people of the United States. And the same is true of our Russian relationships. *The Germans will certainly accuse all three of our European Allies of adopting policies which forced them to war. The reason I say that is that captured documents which we have, always made that claim—that Germany would be forced into war. They admit they were planning war, but the captured documents of the Foreign Office that I have examined all come down to the claim, " We have no way out ; we must fight ; we are encircled ; we are being strangled to death* ".[1] Now, if the question comes up, what is a judge to do about it ? I would say that, before one is judged guilty of being an aggressor we must not only let him deny it, but say we will hear his case. I am quite sure a British or American judge would say to a defendant, " You may prove your claim ", unless we had something like this which says, " No political, military, or other considerations excuse going to war ". In other words, States have got to settle their grievances peacefully. I am afraid there is a great risk in omitting this and I see no risk in putting it in. It may be criticized, but I see no such risk in putting it in as in leaving it out. We did not think it necessary originally, but more recently we have.' (pp. 305, 306).

Is it conceivable that a neutral authority would have even allowed discussion of such a plan to weight the scales of justice against the Vanquished ? Speed, and the avoidance of inconvenient questions, were no doubt important to the Victors but are unconvincing to the layman.

July 25. Six days later we find Mr. Justice Jackson still fighting for his formula : ' Now, however, we propose that no political, economic, or other consideration may be justification for a war of aggression, reserving, of course, the right of legitimate self-defence. As I have said before, our country was so far from this war and we were so late coming in that I am not at all worried, so far as the United States is concerned, about the countercharge that there has been no aggression, because there were acts of Germany's enemies which made the aggression really self-defensive in character. But I don't want to be in a position where the United States is obliged to enter into a discussion at this trial of the acts or policies of our allies. If that arose in the trial, I should withdraw and leave it to be discussed by the powers involved. I think it would be a most unfortunate situation if the trial became involved in the political policies that lay back of the war. Too many recriminations would result. And why should the court stop it if we four men are not willing to stop it ? There is much more justification for us to stop it than for the court to stop it, and it seems to me this trial is likely to take a very unfortunate course if we don't so

---

[1] Author's italics.

limit it that it does not get into the remote causes of the war.'
(pp. 380, 381).

Surely the Allies had not very much to fear from a thorough
ventilation of the German grievances. We made our mistakes
—some of them are mentioned in Chapter III (though there
were many more), but except the Russian aggressions, there
was nothing very criminal in our record. Even if we did have
something to fear from exposure, that would not justify anything giving an impression of unfairness to men being tried
for their lives and for their country's reputation before a
legal Tribunal. A proper ventilation of the invasion of Norway,
discussed in Chapter IV, would almost certainly have reversed
the decision of the court on that particular issue ; and there
may be other instances of the same kind which have not yet been
fully investigated. It would surely have been worth a great deal
to avoid the shadow of mistrust that is now falling on these trials.

All the time every Delegation, in a spirit of the utmost good-
will, was concocting drafts and redrafts of formulae both oᴀ
' crimes ' and of ' aggression ' in order to try and break the
deadlock. Some contained extraordinary features. A French
draft dated July 19, for example, included the following in a list
of war crimes :

' The policy of aggression against, and of domination over,
other nations, *carried out by the European Axis Powers* in breach of
treaties and in violation of international law.' (p. 293).

This proposal to limit the trial of aggression to the European
Axis Powers was of course a gift to the Russians, who were
suspect of a number of aggressions. The idea was reproduced
in several Soviet drafts (pp. 343, 373), and in two British drafts
which had been prepared to meet the views of the Soviet Delegation. (pp. 359, 392). But Mr. Justice Jackson rejected
every proposal for the sound reason that it was a partisan
declaration of law, and that it would deprive the definition of
all standing and fairness as a juridical principle. That the
proposal should have had the support of three out of the four
Delegations throws a disagreeable light on the atmosphere of
the discussions.

During the final discussion of the definition of aggression on
July 25, when all sorts of last moment ideas had been thrown
out, the Russian Delegate (whose attitude had throughout been

helpful and constructive on this issue) made the following
laconic statement :—

' Is it proposed then to condemn aggression or initiation of
war in general or to condemn specifically aggressions started
by the Nazis in this war ? If the attempt is to have a general
definition, that would not be agreeable.' (p. 387). He at
least had learned from the past—Litvinov's Definition, so
promptly broken, must have haunted him.

However, no acceptable definition could be found. When
someone tried to raise it again later on General Nikitshenko
observed dryly : ' If we start on that again, I am afraid the
war criminals would all die of old age ! ' A little later still
Mr. Justice Jackson repeated once more his main thesis and
concluded :—

' Maybe you will have judges who without such provision
would rule such matter out ; but, if I were sitting and you
objected to their political or economic justification, I would say
you were drawing the agreement. If you thought it an illegal
defence, why did you not say so ? '

General Nikitshenko : ' The judges perhaps would be experienced enough to consider that as irrelevant.' (p. 389).

And that is what happened. At many of the German Trials
much of the evidence on which the defendants had relied was
ruled out as irrelevant. Exactly how that was managed history
does not record, but Article 18 of the Charter laid down that:—

The Tribunal shall

(a) confine the Trial strictly to an expeditious hearing of the
     issues raised by the charges,
(b) take strict measures to prevent any action which will cause
     unreasonable delay, and rule out irrelevant issues and
     statements of any kind whatsoever.

No doubt a great deal could be done with those powers.
But the real question is ' Will it satisfy the present or future
generations that the trials were fair ? Was it politically wise ? '

It is perhaps worth mentioning that, rightly or wrongly, I
had heard that I was on a German list of allied war criminals.
I therefore watched these trials closely and saw from the first
that the only possible line of defence on these political charges—
and not a bad defence if properly handled—was to raise these
very issues which the authors of the Charter were so anxious

to exclude. And, nursed on our traditions of the rule of law and of fair trial, I observed their exclusion with astonishment.

It is interesting to recall that nearly a year before the London Conference the whole question of the German Peace arrangements, including the Trial of the War Criminals, was being considered in the United States. About that time the President and Mr. Hull asked Mr. James Byrnes to consider becoming the American High Commissioner for Germany. There was at the time considerable difference of opinion in the American Cabinet on the general issue and Mr. Byrnes was shown the papers. ' One provision,' he records, ' struck me particularly. Its phraseology was tantamount to saying that the principal war criminals should be tried and hanged. I asked if consideration had been given to the possibility that some of those charged might be acquitted or that a mistrial might occur. . . . Shortly thereafter, I informed the President and Secretary Hull that I could not accept the appointment, since I did not think I was qualified for the task.' [1]

No one who has read the above brief digest of the London Conference, 1945, will be surprised at his decision.

Observations

We have seen why the London Conference of 1945 was unable to arrive at a definition of aggression. There are, however, considerations of a more general character that make an accurate definition impracticable. The principal of these is that there is usually some provocation for an aggression and it is often impossible to judge the point at which a provocation becomes itself an aggression. That difficulty is particularly liable to arise in connection with the maltreatment of minorities of different nationality and/or religion from that of the majority of a population. If that maltreatment reaches the point of massacre or threat to human life, no definition of aggression will prevent a powerful country from intervening to protect its co-nationals or co-religionists. In the judgement of history, who would call this an aggression ?

Sometimes also a technical aggression may have to be undertaken for the protection of minorities in case of the inability of a Government, through civil war or sheer inefficiency, lack of

[1] James F. Byrnes, *Speaking Frankly*, pp. 183–4.

the will or the means to keep order in its own territories. It has never been found possible to devise a definition that will provide for all the different contingencies that are liable to arise in history, and to-day the subject is more difficult than ever owing to the disruptive and weakening effects on Governments of ideologies like Communism and to the theoretical equality of all countries, to say nothing of the ease of aggression by air forces, submarine mines, V1 and V2 weapons and the like. Who, for example, could have foreseen the very peculiar circumstances of Admiral Somerville's attack on Mers-el-Kebir mentioned above? Yet, in modern war, which under the present drift towards ‘ internationalization ’ is nearly certain to become a world war (no more ‘ ringing wars round ’, as so often in the past), the complications are certain to become more numerous and the act of aggression more difficult to determine.

One of the main lessons to be drawn from the events referred to so far—and fully developed in later chapters—is the fact that threats like Unconditional Surrender and Trials of War Criminals are a mistake in war. If for some reason they cannot be avoided, the announcement should be withheld until the last possible moment. Before the announcement that nothing but Unconditional Surrender would satisfy the Allies there were signs of disillusionment in Germany : but those almost disappeared after the announcement at Casablanca. Within a month of the announcement Goebbels (whose Diary mostly contains more realism than boastfulness) was congratulating himself day after day on the success of his propaganda (March 1, 4, 6, 7, 9, 11; April 28, 29, etc.), both at home and in enemy countries, especially in causing dissension among the Allies. And after the announcement of the companion policy of War Crimes Trials at Moscow on November 1 the Diary has many references to hatred of England (due partly, of course, to air raids), the great success of Hitler's speech of November 9, ‘ no longer any talk in the English press of moral collapse in the Reich ’ (November 11, 1943), and so forth. In an article in *Das Reich* as late as July, 1944, he said : ‘ Our enemies made a major blunder by forcing on Germany a war with the issue of life and death ’.

Of the surrender of Italy Goebbels wrote—‘ No traitorous clique of generals ever signed a more shameless document.

The conditions of the armistice are dishonourable and humiliating '.
(September 13, 1943). By the enforcement of unconditional
surrender on Italy, a nation that had come to us to offer friendship and co-operation, any hope that might have existed of a
normal peace settlement disappeared. On September 3, 1943,
for example, Goebbels asked the Fuehrer whether he would be
ready to negotiate with Churchill or whether he declined this
on principle. ' The Fuehrer replied that in politics principles
simply do not exist when it comes to questions of personalities.
He does not believe that negotiations with Churchill would lead
to any result as he is too deeply wedded to his hostile views, and,
besides is guided by hatred and not by reason.' It is curious
that Mr. Churchill has stated that ' Negotiation with Hitler
was impossible. He was a maniac with supreme power to play
his hand out to the end, which he did, and so did we '.[1] This
is a good example of the state of mind to which policies of
hate lead.

Surely, however, if it had not been for these deadly policies
some means would have been found, as in nearly all the wars of
history, to end the business without the frightful calamities of
the last two years of hostilities. There would probably have
been no need at all to negotiate with Hitler, as one of the conditions of the Allies, after they had gained the upper hand,
would have been the disappearance of Hitler and his gang. A
German ' Badoglio ' would certainly have been found, as in
the case of Italy, had it not been for these fatal pronouncements.
We need but read Hassell's *Diaries* to get to know many such
men ready to destroy Hitler and his works for the sake of their
country and the peace of the world.

Had an earlier peace been possible, either after the Italian
surrender or later, what a difference it would have made !
Months, possibly years of the most bitter warfare, huge casualty
figures and great losses would have been avoided : the deep
separation of the Western Powers from Russia might never have
taken place : neither France, Belgium, Holland, Luxembourg,
nor Germany and Italy would have suffered such appalling
devastation from the continuous attacks of allied aircraft : the
nations east of the present Iron Curtain might never have been
annexed or fallen under the domination of the U.S.S.R. : had

[1] *The White House Papers*, Vol. II, p. 692.

we but had the sense to drop Unconditional Surrender and the policy of War Crimes Trials—as I urged—we might long ago have made a reasonable peace with all our former foes.

In addition, we should have avoided the lasting odium of these political trials, which, owing to the difference between the jurisprudence of the nations concerned, however praiseworthy the efforts of the judges, could not reach the highest standard of justice, or command the confidence either of present or future generations. Nothing was lost by the abandonment of the trials in 1920, and nothing but good would have come from their abandonment before or after the end of World War II.

The following extract from the dissenting opinion of Judge Radhabinode Pal of the Calcutta High Court, the representative of India on the Tokyo Tribunal, illustrates this point :—

' The so-called Trial held according to the definition of crime now given by the victors obliterates the centuries of civilization which stretch between us and the summary slaying of the defeated in a war. A trial with law thus prescribed will only be a sham employment of legal process for the satisfaction of a thirst for revenge. It does not correspond to any idea of justice (and) may justly create the feeling that it is much more a political than a legal affair . . . . To say that the victor can define a crime at his will . . . and then punish . . . would be to revert back to those days when he was allowed to devastate the occupied country, . . . appropriate all public and private property therein, and kill the inhabitants or take them away into captivity . . . '

To sum up, war is an extension of policy, though a most deplorable and regrettable one, to be avoided or at least to be postponed as long as at all possible. But when all prophylactics have failed and it can no longer be avoided it must be faced like abnormalities of nature, earthquakes, epidemic diseases, famine or drought. The first aim in war is to win, the second to avoid defeat, the third to shorten it, and the fourth and the most important, which must never be lost to sight, is to make a just and durable peace. Emotionalism of all kinds, hate, revenge, punishment and anything that handicaps the nation in achieving these four aims are out of place. It must always be kept in mind that after a war we have sooner or later to live with our enemies in amity. To quote the classics once more :—

' For the purpose with which good men wage wars is not the destruction and annihilation of the wrongdoers, but the reformation and alteration of the wrongful acts. Nor is it their object to involve the innocent in the destruction of the guilty, but rather to see that those who are held to be guilty should share in the preservation and elevation of the guiltless '.[1]

That, of course, is a pagan pronouncement. But it sets a standard that the Allies never even approached in the Second World War ! We prided ourselves on possessing a higher moral code, a more Christian spirit than the Germans and Japanese. We avoided the degradations of human cruelty to which those nations fell, but we did commit the errors of threatening and carrying into execution Unconditional Surrender and the War Crimes Trials. In addition, we stretched retaliation to extreme limits. Not content with an eye for an eye, and a tooth for a tooth, we must have dropped a hundred bombs for one bomb. It may be said that one wrong makes another right in war— that is the underlying principle of retaliation—but there ought to be some limit to the scale, especially where the civilian population are the principal victims. That limit, surely must have been exceeded by the Atomic Bomb to which we shall return in a later chapter.

[1] The *Histories of Polybius.* Book V. Ch. II.

CHAPTER TWO

THE POLITICS OF
UNCONDITIONAL SURRENDER

As to the parentage and date and birthplace of Unconditional Surrender, there is no doubt. The idea was President Roosevelt's and no one is likely to contest it. He produced it on Saturday, January 23, 1943, in his villa at Casablanca, while lunching with Mr. Winston Churchill, Mr. Harry Hopkins, the President's confidant and friend, and his son, Elliott Roosevelt, who noted this important event in his diary. According to that account Mr. Churchill thought, frowned, thought, finally grinned and at length announced 'Perfect . . .'. Later on he proposed the toast of ' Unconditional Surrender ', which they all drank. That was all.

It would be expected that such an all important decision would at once have been referred for examination and report to the highest military authorities, who were gathered at Casablanca in considerable numbers—the Combined Chiefs of Staff, the British and United States Joint Chiefs of Staff, Commanders-in-Chief from every theatre of war by sea, by land, and in the air—to concert the plans for the next stages of the war. There is no evidence, however, that they were consulted or told anything about it. General Eisenhower, who visited Casablanca during the Conference, only heard of it after his return to Algiers. Everyone was busy. The Conference was to end next day. The Allied Service representatives were putting the finishing touches on the far-reaching strategical plans that the Combined Staffs had been hammering out for ten days. A telegram had to be drafted to inform Marshal Stalin, who had excused himself since he was too busy to come to Casablanca. The Prime Minister and the President were still working on the Press Communique that night, and the President had to devote the next morning to a reconciliation between General Giraud and General de Gaulle.

At noon on the next day, Sunday, January 24, 1943, less than twenty-four hours after he had propounded the idea, the President, apparently without further warning to Mr. Churchill, announced it to the press of the world assembled in the garden of the villa where he and Mr. Churchill were seated side by side in the warm African sunshine.

The fact is that the communique itself was a bit thin—not very substantial pabulum for press-men who had come so far and were in a state of high expectancy. The work of the Conference had been of major military importance ; but policy and plans were necessarily secret and not much could be said about them to the press even ' off the record '. Unconditional Surrender, therefore, provided a useful make-weight to the colourless communique. Yet—what a lot of trouble, and how many human lives, how much destruction and what misery would have been saved if that had been kept a secret too : better still, if it had never been accepted as a worthy war aim.

The President spoke first. When he felt that his story of the Conference was falling rather flat he suddenly turned to the future, to something which he said ' had always been in the heart and minds of people, but never before placed on paper. That was that peace would only come by the elimination of German and Japanese war power '.[1] Then, turning to the British correspondents, he told them how in the American civil war General U. S. Grant had won the nickname of ' Unconditional Surrender Grant '.

' Unconditional surrender, to-day, Mr. Roosevelt explained with emphasis, meant unconditional surrender by Germany, Italy, and Japan, and that meant a reasonable assurance of world peace. It did not mean, he explained, the destruction of the populations of these countries, but the destruction of the philosophies in those countries based on fear and hate and the subjugation of other peoples.'[2]

How often has the attempt been made to destroy philosophies and religions by threats and by force and how seldom has it succeeded !

At that point ' as it were a happy thought that had just entered his mind ' the President threw out the suggestion that

[1] The London *Times* special correspondent, January 27, 1943.
Ibid.

the Casablanca Conference should be known as the ' Unconditional Surrender Meeting ', which Mr. Churchill greeted with a very English ' hear, hear '[1] Beyond that ejaculation and brief general support to the principle of Unconditional Surrender the Prime Minister added little to what the President had said on the subject and for the rest confined himself to a brilliant review of the military situation.

But those two words were enough. Within a few minutes that announcement was hurtling round the world by cable and wireless to Foreign Offices, Cabinets, Parliaments, Chancelleries, War Offices, G. H.Q's., newspaper offices, to be blazoned forth in the largest headlines, to broadcasting stations and to the homes of the people, bringing—it was thought—hope to the Allies, while hardening the hearts of their enemies, fanning the flames of bitterness and hate and postponing peace to the Greek Kalends !

Mr. Churchill's Attitude

Study of the published accounts soon showed that Mr. Churchill had been less enthusiastic about unconditional surrender than Mr. Roosevelt. It was remarked that the official communiqué on the Conference issued by the Ministry of Information in time for the newspapers of January 27 did not mention the subject at all. In the House of Commons on February 11, 1943, the Prime Minister was almost apologetic. In a speech of more than twenty columns of *Hansard*, unconditional surrender appears in the sixth column and the subject occupies only twenty-eight lines. At the outset he emphasized that ' *the President* '[2] ' with my full concurrence as agent of the War Cabinet, *decided* that the note of the Casablanca Conferences, should be the unconditional surrender of all our foes.' And again, at the end of this passage the Prime Minister brought out unmistakably that it was the President's initiative :—

" That disposes, I think, of two important features of the Casablanca Conference, the defeat of the U-boat . . . and secondly, *the statement which the President wished to be made on the subject of unconditional surrender.*"[3]

[1] The London *Times* special correspondent, January 27, 1943.
[2] Author's italics.
[3] *Hansard*, Commons, February 11, 1943, col. 692.

That preliminary impression has since been confirmed. For Mr. Robert Sherwood, the editor of the *White House Papers*, afterwards wrote to Mr. Churchill asking him if he had discussed the statement with the President before the Press Conference and received a reply (pp. 692–3) to the effect that the Prime Minister had heard the words 'Unconditional Surrender' for the first time from the President's lips at the Conference. He would not have used those words himself, but immediately stood by the President and afterwards frequently defended the decision. It is also mentioned that the President himself absolved Churchill from all responsibility for the statement and suggested that it was unpremeditated on his own part.

Mr. Churchill's attitude, however, was placed beyond all possible doubt in the House of Commons on July 21, 1949, when, replying to Mr. Bevin, who had revealed that " neither the British Cabinet nor any other Cabinet had a chance to say a word before the adoption of the formula " he spoke as follows:—

" The statement was made by President Roosevelt without consultation with me. I was there on the spot, and I had very rapidly to consider whether the state of our position in the world was such as would justify me in not giving support to it. I did give support to it, but that was not the idea which I had formed in my own mind. In the same way, when it came to the Cabinet at home, I have not the slightest doubt that if the British Cabinet had considered that phrase, it is likely that they would have advised against it, but working with a great alliance and with great, loyal and powerful friends from across the ocean, we had to accommodate ourselves."

In fairness to Mr. Churchill also it ought to be remembered that he had got his way about the strategy: that is to say the favourable situation in North Africa and the Mediterranean was to be exploited to the full before operation Overlord, the invasion of Normandy, was undertaken. Had he opposed the President's pet project he might have jeopardized his success by upsetting the atmosphere. Still, as we shall see later in this Chapter the results were deplorable, and whoever was responsible a snap decision on such a far-reaching subject was one of the gravest errors of the war.

Marshal Stalin's Attitude

Marshal Stalin was not consulted beforehand about this momentous decision, but was at once informed. Although at the luncheon-table on January 23, according to Mr. Elliott Roosevelt, the President thought that unconditional surrender would be just the thing for the Russians, there is evidence that Stalin did not at first take kindly to the idea. During the Washington Conference in May, 1943 (known in America as the Trident Conference), according to the *White House Papers* Mr. Roosevelt decided to issue a statement to define the Unconditional Surrender formula; it meant that the United Nations would never negotiate an armistice with the Nazi Government, the German High Command, or any other organization or group or individual in Germany. But he dropped the idea because Mr. Churchill dissuaded him on the ground that Stalin would not have agreed on that point, though he would have agreed with Roosevelt that Germany could not be defeated by anything less than the application of overwhelming armed forces on the continent itself in the West.[1]

Further evidence is available from the fact that the warning given to Germany's satellites—Hungary, Roumania, Bulgaria and Finland by Great Britain, the United States and Russia on May 12, 1944, as to the risks they were running by submitting to the German occupation, made no mention of Unconditional Surrender. The well-informed Diplomatic Correspondent of the *Daily Telegraph* stated, first in a forecast of the coming statement on May 9, and later in an account of it on May 13, that the original formula of Unconditional Surrender was modified under Stalin's influence. Later, however, as Germany weakened he became reconciled to the formula, which, by prolonging the war and weakening his Allies, enabled him to over-run and dominate the whole of Eastern Europe as had long been planned by him.

The Meaning of the Formula

On February 11, 1943, in the course of his short mention in Parliament of Unconditional Surrender already quoted on page 30, Mr. Churchill added :

'But our inflexible insistence upon unconditional surrender

[1] *The White House Papers*, p. 285.

does not mean that we shall stain our victorious arms by any cruel treatment of whole populations. But justice must be done upon the wicked and the guilty, and, within her proper bounds, justice must be stern and implacable. No vestige of the Nazi or Fascist power, no vestige of the Japanese war plotting machine will be left to us when the work is done, and done it certainly will be.'[1]

We see here the beginning of the policy of War Crimes Trials, the natural sequel to Unconditional Surrender, which was announced later in the year, but it is noteworthy that as yet justice was to be kept ' within her proper bounds '—a prescient phrase!

Two days later (February 13) in a broadcast, President Roosevelt spoke as follows :

' In an attempt to ward off inevitable disaster, the Axis propagandists are trying all of their old tricks in order to divide the United Nations. They seek to create the idea that if we win this war, Russia, England, China and the United States are going to get into a cat and dog fight.' (That was prophetic).

' That is their final effort to turn one nation against another in the vain hope that they may settle with one or two at a time. . . .'

' To these panicky attempts to escape the consequences of their crimes we say—all the United Nations—say that the only terms on which we shall deal with any Axis Government or any Axis factions are the terms proclaimed at Casablanca : " *Unconditional Surrender* " '.

' In our uncompromising policy we mean no harm to common people of the Axis nations. But we do mean to impose punishment upon the guilty, barbaric leaders '.

In those last words the War Crimes policy was again foreshadowed. But, so far, it was confined to the leaders.

In time a good deal of doubt began to assert itself about the policy of ' unconditional surrender ', and on February 22, 1944, Mr. Churchill sought to clarify it further :

' Here I may point out that the term " Unconditional Surrender " does not mean that the German people will be enslaved or destroyed. It means, however, that the Allies will

---

[1] *Hansard*, February 11, 1943.

not be bound to them at the moment of surrender by any pact or obligation. There will be, for instance, no question of the Atlantic Charter applying to Germany as a matter of right and banning territorial transferences or adjustments in any countries.'

That statement seems to overlook the fact that the various clauses in the Atlantic Charter applied severally to ' all peoples', ' all States, great or small, *victor or vanquished* '[1], (viz., ' access on equal terms to trade and raw materials'), ' all nations ' and ' all men '. By this new statement the enemy States were deprived of any prospect of sharing automatically the benefits of the Atlantic Charter which became a distant guerdon on the far side of Unconditional Surrender. To continue Mr. Churchill's subsequent explanation :

' No such arguments will be admitted by us as were used by Germany after the last war, saying that they surrendered in consequence of President Wilson's Fourteen Points. Unconditional Surrender means that the victors have a free hand. It does not mean that they are entitled to behave in a barbarous manner, nor that they wish to blot out Germany from among the nations of Europe. If we are bound, we are bound by our own consciences to civilization. We are not to be bound as the result of a bargain struck. That is the meaning of " Unconditional Surrender " '.[2]

Thus more than a year after the declaration our Leaders were still trying to think out what it meant. But what would they have found if they had taken the trouble to look into the question before they took the plunge ?

Unconditional Surrender in Roman History

There must be historical records of many demands for ' unconditional surrender ' of besieged cities, and beleaguered armies, but instances of the application of the formula to organized States are few and far between. In ancient times Carthage provides the most interesting (but not the only) example. In the year 150 B.C. the Carthaginians were reported to be rearming in contravention of the Treaty (of 201 B.C.) which had

---

[1] Author's italics.
[2] *Hansard*, Commons, February 22, 1944, Col. 699.

been imposed upon them after the second Punic War. Hard pressed by the African King Massanissa, Rome's watchdog over the execution of the Treaty, they sent Commissioners to discuss their difficulties in Rome. Finding on arrival that war (for which Rome had been seeking a pretext) had already been decreed and that Roman forces were on the way to Africa, the envoys offered ' Unconditional Surrender '. Polybius tells us that the Roman definition of that phrase was very stiff ; it included surrender of all territory and cities and of all men and women therein, as well as of rivers, harbours, temples and tombs.

However, the Senate at first granted the Carthaginians easier terms than that—their freedom and enjoyment of their own laws, all their territory and the possession of their other property, public and private, in return for the surrender of 300 young hostages of the best families. After some hesitation these were handed over. Soon after, however, a Roman fleet arrived off shore and collected 200,000 stands of arms and 2,000 catapults. Having, as they thought, disarmed their enemy the Romans next insisted on the whole population of Carthage moving inland, at least ten miles from the sea, and building a new city there.

This proved the last straw. The Carthaginians decided to resist to the death. As nearly always follows from such extortionate demands, there followed one of the most bitter campaigns of history, accompanied by brutality and suffering. It lasted from 149 to 146 B.C., when the city was stormed, sacked, and burned.[1]

English History

English history appears to record no case of a demand for ' Unconditional Surrender ' before 1943 ! Fifteen major wars since the end of the sixteenth century have been examined in some detail to support this statement. Nearly all our major wars in Europe involved continental nations as well, either as enemies or allies, and, in accordance with the usual practice these wars were brought to an end by the conclusion of a Peace

[1] The *Histories of Polybius* also record an instance of a Roman interpretation of ' Unconditional Surrender ' applied to the Greek State of Aetolia in 191 B.C. ; this, too, was so drastic that the inhabitants refused to discuss it and dropped their peace overture. (Book XX. Ch. 9).

Treaty. Rarely, therefore, has there been such a long delay in peace making as has followed the ' Unconditional Surrender ' War which ended in 1945.

The South African War

Early in 1901, however, during the war in South Africa, a controversy blew up on the subject between Lord Kitchener, the British Commander-in-Chief in South Africa, and Lord Milner, the High Commissioner. Kitchener had proposed to meet General Botha to discuss possible terms of peace ; but Lord Milner, the High Commissioner, held that negotiation was premature and that Unconditional Surrender was vital, if the idea of racial domination was to be uprooted once and for all. Neither of these tenacious personalities would give way, and the Home Government had to intervene and settle the issue. They came down against Unconditional Surrender. As Mr. Joseph Chamberlain wrote to Lord Milner (with whose views he nevertheless had much sympathy) ' there seems to be a flavour of medieval cruelty about Unconditional Surrender from which we shrink '.

The terms which Kitchener was able to offer, however, proved too stiff for Botha to accept, and the war continued for fifteen months longer. In spite of the good sense of the British Government in rejecting the formula the mere fact that it had been mentioned left a legacy of bitterness in South Africa and was long remembered. Even General Botha, a paragon of magnanimity, as late as the Paris Peace Conference could not speak of Unconditional Surrender without exasperation.

World War I

In World War I the formula of Unconditional Surrender was never mentioned until the last month. Almost from the first day of the war our peace aims were clearly defined, and Unconditional Surrender was never included nor even discussed. Mr. Asquith's pithy summary of our aims at the Guildhall, in November, 1914, would be hard to beat :

' We shall never sheathe the sword which we have not lightly drawn until Belgium recovers in full measure all and more than all that she has sacrificed, until France is adequately secured against the menace of aggression, until the rights of the smaller nationalities of Europe are placed upon an unassailable foundation and until the domination of Prussia is wholly and finally destroyed '.

On that basis, endorsed and slightly supplemented by M. Viviani, the French Prime Minister, on December 22, 1919, the peace aims were overhauled from time to time to meet war developments such as the entry of Turkey, Bulgaria, Italy, and eventually the United States of America into the war. During 1917 revised statements were announced more than once as the result of deliberations by the Imperial War Cabinet and the principal Allies, but Mr. Asquith's basic principles were never upset. Early in January, 1918, President Wilson announced his Fourteen Points, which, with some interpretations and reservations on details, became the accepted basis of the peace *pourparlers* in the autumn of 1918.

Up to this moment the question of ' surrender '—let alone ' unconditional surrender ' had never been brought up. But in his third note to the German Government on the subject of the armistice President Wilson, after expressing lack of confidence in the professed change of Government in Germany, added : if the United States had to deal ' with the military masters and monarchical autocrats of Germany now, or if it is likely to have to deal with them later, in regard to the international obligations of the German Empire, it must demand, *not peace negotiations but surrender* '.

The rest of the story I summarized in my account of the episode to the House of Lords on May 26, 1944, as follows :

" That produced a tremendous effect. Hindenburg and Ludendorff reacted violently. Throwing over their earlier demands for peace negotiations, they drafted and signed a telegram headed ' For the information of all Troops ' in which they described President Wilson's Note as a demand for Unconditional Surrender. ' It is thus unacceptable to us soldiers '. The draft telegram concluded with an appeal ' to continue our resistance with all our strength ! ' But they were too late. The German Government was irrevocably committed to peace and the telegram was never sent ".

Once more then, we see the effect that this deadly phrase can have on a warring nation, and how near it came to

prolonging the war in 1918.   For Unconditional Surrender is
a policy of despair, and as a German proverb says : ' Despair
gives courage to a coward ' ; or as a French proverb puts it :
' *Le désespoir redouble nos forces* ' ; or to quote Montaigne : ' It is
one of the grestest discretions in the rule of war not to drive an
enemy to despair. . . 'Tis dangerous to attack a man you have
deprived of all means to escape but by his arms, for necessity
teaches violent resolutions. . . .'.[1]

All this history even ' old saws ', indeed much more of both,
were brushed aside when the President and the less enthusiastic Prime Minister made their portentous announcement of
Unconditional Surrender on that bright Sunday morning at
Casablanca in January, 1943.

Italy and Unconditional Surrender in World War II

We come now to the story of the application of unconditional
surrender in World War II, when, in one country after another
the bad results of this policy repeated themselves.   Italy was
the first of our enemies to collapse and to Italy we turn first.

The insistence of the British and American Governments
on the application of the Unconditional Surrender formula to
Italy deserves careful study.   It brings out well the disadvantages and embarrassments which it must cause to the conduct
of military operations as well as to the making of peace.   The
adoption of this rigid principle in war leads to disastrous and
tragic consequences.   In June and July, 1943, as part of the
process of ' softening ' Italy, a good deal of propaganda was
carried out.   The first part of the story, which began well, is
best told in the terms of a speech I delivered in the House of
Lords on September 23, 1943 :

" The story begins . . . with a broadcast that was made from
Algiers on July 15 in the names of the President of the United
States and the Prime Minister of the United Kingdom.   That
broadcast made no mention of the term Unconditional Surrender.   Much less humiliating phraseology was used, and I
hope your Lordships will allow me to quote from it : ' The
sole hope for Italy's survival lies in *honourable capitulation* to the

---

[1] Essays of Montaigne. ' Uncertainty of our Judgement '.

overwhelming power of the military forces of the United Nations'.[1]

" I felt when I read that very fine document that it was an extraordinarily nice stroke substituting ' honourable capitulation ' for ' unconditional surrender '. I know the Italians very well, because I have dealt with them both in the last war and at many international conferences. They are an extraordinarily sensitive people. They have got a very fine sense of honour, and are very much influenced often by what to us rather tough people does not matter very much. There is all the difference, I can assure your Lordships, to the Italians— and I can think of other nations as well—between ' unconditional surrender ' and ' honourable capitulation '.

" That document was in effect a powerful but persuasive appeal to the Italian people, first to capitulate, then to get rid of Mussolini and the Fascist régime, and finally to get rid of the Germans. The effect of that appeal, of which I have no criticism to make—combined with the advance in Sicily and the bombing of Italy—was very remarkable. Within ten days the second part of the advice had been taken. Mussolini was deposed, Badoglio reigned in his stead, and the Fascist régime was abolished.

" At the end of July other statements were made on rather similar lines. On July 29 President Roosevelt made a broadcast, and while he did once use the phrase ' unconditional surrender ', it was rather persuasive, rather holding out hopes to the Italians. He expressed the determination of the Allies to restore these conquered peoples to the dignity of human beings, masters of their own fate, entitled to freedom of speech, freedom of religion, freedom from want and freedom from fear.

" On the very same day, in a broadcast to the Italians, General Eisenhower spoke in much the same vein. In urging them to get rid of the Germans, he made it clear that they could have peace immediately ' on the honourable conditions that our Governments have laid down '. I thought, and still think, that that was a throw-back to the ' honourable capitu-

[1] From the *White House Papers* we know now that the broadcast had been drafted a month earlier, and that extraordinary efforts were made to get its message home to the Italian people by powerful radio establishments in North Africa and by millions of leaflets dropped from aeroplanes. (p. 737).

lation' mentioned in the statement of July 15. In his next
sentence he struck possibly an even better note. He said, ' we
are coming as liberators '. The relentless bombing of the
armies in Sicily and the bombing of the mainland had strongly
disinclined the Italians from continuing the war. . . . They
were disinclined, especially when the bombing was combined
with the sweeping advances of the Allied Armies through Sicily
and with the series of statements which I have quoted, admirably supported by the kindliness of our soldiers and airmen,
who are really our best diplomats. All these things were
showing the Italians that an honourable capitulation was within
reach. It was not therefore very unexpected when, in the first
week of August, feelers were put out by the Italian Government.

"That seems to me to have been a particularly decisive
moment. A great opportunity was opened up. After all, the
main object of our policy was, and is (I was speaking in 1943),
to defeat the Germans ; and here was an occasion, which might
with luck, be used not only to eliminate our enemy's principal
ally, Italy, but even to get them on our side, to get the whole-
hearted good will of the whole nation before Germany had time
to increase to strangling point her growing grip on the country.
At that moment also we were dealing with Marshal Badoglio,
a soldier who is notoriously anti-German, a good colleague in
the last war, a man who had taken all risks in upsetting Mussolini and the Fascist régime, a man who had already carried out,
at great risk, the second advice of July 15, by making his
approach with a view to honourable capitulation and with a
view to opposing the Germans. We had not the slightest
reason to doubt his good faith."

What, meanwhile, happened in Italy ? Marshal Badoglio,
the new Head of the Government, was setting about making
peace. His policy is made clear in his book, *Italy in the Second
World War*, where he explains the views he then held :

' I was also sure that if I could get into touch with the Allies
I could obtain better terms than the Unconditional Surrender
on which the English continued to insist.' (p. 56).

It is remarkable that Great Britain had by then come to be
considered the stickler for what hitherto had been regarded
by many as Roosevelt's pet fad. There is some confirmation

for this Italian view in the *White House Papers*. It is there stated
that Mr. Churchill was furious because ' the pyschological
warriors in North Africa ' had been assuring the Italians (by
radio) that their prisoners of war would be returned if they
would surrender ' honourably '. (p. 740). There was also
some pressure in the British parliament for the Unconditional
Surrender of Italy.

On July 29, Badoglio met his new Foreign Minister, Signor
Guariglia. Before leaving his former post at Constantinople
Guariglia had asked the Turkish Foreign Minister to let the
British and United States Ambassadors know his conviction
that Italy was on the point of changing her policy. The Allies
were thus forewarned. The two Ministers, however, encountered difficulties in finding a way of establishing communications with the Allies, since the British and American
Missions to the Vatican had no safe means of communication.
Yet, it was vital to avoid all risk of the Germans discovering
what was afoot. The best plan they could devise was to take
advantage of a special train due to leave Rome with some
Foreign Office Officials for Lisbon on August 12 to send a
General and a representative of the Italian Foreign Office to
that capital. This involved a delay of a fortnight before they
could set off, and it was only on August 15 that they reached
Madrid, where they saw the British Ambassador, Lord Temple-
wood, then Sir Samuel Hoare. The latter at once reported to
Quebec where President Roosevelt and Mr. Churchill had met
so as to be available to settle any proposal that might arrive :
it was to the effect that Italy was willing to make unconditional
surrender, if she could thereby join the Allies.

But that promising proposal received a very lukewarm reception. On August 17 the President and Prime Minister
decided, and informed Marshal Stalin, that they did not propose to bargain with Badoglio's Government in order to induce
Italy to change sides. They recognized, however, that for the
purpose of accelerating surrender operations in Italy would be
useful. The campaign would therefore begin ; meanwhile
General Eisenhower was authorized to send emissaries to Lisbon.

Consequently, when the Italian General Castellano met
General Bedell Smith, General Eisenhower's Chief of Staff, and
a British Officer at Lisbon on August 19, all he got was a

repetition of the phrase Unconditional Surrender and a copy of military ' Terms of Armistice '—to be accepted or rejected ! As he had to spend several days at Lisbon in hiding, for fear he should be discovered by the Germans, before the departure of his train, he only reached Rome on August 28. A whole month had elapsed since Badoglio had first discussed peace with his Foreign Minister ; and the Allies, though they knew that something was afoot had done nothing to shorten the period. The military Armistice Terms were found by Marshal Badoglio to be very harsh and in some instances could not possibly be carried out. So General Castellano was sent off to Sicily, as had been arranged, to see General Bedell Smith, who refused to modify the terms : if they were not accepted, much heavier conditions would be imposed, all the main Italian cities, including Rome, would be razed to the ground and all the Italian industries destroyed. That, at any rate, is Marshal Badoglio's account. (pp. 70–71). On his return Badoglio, Guariglia, General Ambrosio, the Chief of the Italian General Staff, and General Castellano conferred and decided that the military Armistice must be signed. And signed it was on September 3, 1943. But it could not yet be announced or executed because Marshal Badoglio was unwilling to accept it before the Allies had landed at least fifteen divisions on the mainland of Italy to keep the Germans occupied ; this would not be done for some time. Eventually, however, the Marshal was presuaded to agree to the publication of the surrrender on September 8, long before his condition was fulfilled, and he comments that :

' General Eisenhower showed from that moment such an understanding of our needs, such compassion for the fate of our unfortunate country, as to compensate for the troubles and the sufferings which this hasty decision caused us '. (p. 73).

If something of the same spirit had been displayed on the highest levels at Quebec and elsewhere, both before and after the announcement of the armistice, one cannot help feeling that better results would have been achieved.

One thing, however, had been secured in the terms of the military armistice to which Marshal Badoglio attached great importance : *there was no mention of Unconditional Surrender.* Neither was the phrase used in the announcement of the

Armistice, which was issued in the following terms : ' Recognizing the impossibility of continuing the war in face of the overwhelming strength of the enemy, and in order to save the nation from further and even greater disasters, the Italian Government has asked General Eisenhower, Commander-in-Chief of the Allied Forces, for an armistice.

' This request has been acceded to.

' In consequence all hostilities by the Italian armed forces against the British and American forces must now cease. They will, however, repel attacks from whatever quarter they may come.'

One would have expected that what was good enough for General Eisenhower would be good enough for the Home Authorities. But, having committed themselves to the disastrous formula of Unconditional Surrender, the politicians deemed it necessary to try and force it down the throat of the very man who was doing his utmost to bring Italy into full co-operation with the Allies! On or about September 20, more than a fortnight after the armistice had been signed, the political representatives handed to Marshal Badoglio the completed text of the Armistice, which included the military, political, and administrative clauses, which it had always been understood would come later. To his astonishment and dismay the Marshal found that the document was entitled ' *The Unconditional Surrender of Italy* '. After stating in a preamble that the Allied Governments had accepted *the unconditional surrender of Italy*, it set forth the demands made in forty-four articles. The Marshal, according to his own account (p. 95) then told the political representatives that General Castellano had never agreed to an Unconditional Surrender. The intrusion of this phrase was a subterfuge which might have been forgiven had it been resorted to by a defeated nation in the hope of escaping too heavy penalties, but it was ungenerous and dishonourable on the part of victors whom the defeated nation was now assisting. To this the reply of the embarrassed Allied representatives was that they had not drafted the document, and that, before the Marshal signed it he had better discuss it at a forthcoming interview with General Eisenhower. On that day, September 20, as I noted at the time, Marshal

Badoglio broadcast a statement that included the following :
' Do not forget that all talk of unconditional surrender is out of
date and irrelevant to the changed conditions of to-day.'

On September 28, Marshal Badoglio, accompanied by General
Sir Frank Mason-MacFarlane, who seems to have comported
himself with the utmost tact and circumspection, left Brindisi
for Malta to see General Eisenhower. The Marshal at once
broached the question of the addition of Unconditional Surrender to the military armistice signed on September 3, which
was admitted to be still in force. After reciting what Italy had
done to carry out the terms of the armistice and General
Eisenhower's demands he asked point blank what was the
justification for the severity of the new terms and the addition
of conditions that were disadvantageous to Italy and *humiliating*.

Eisenhower, Bedell Smith, and Mason-MacFarlane, at the
latter's suggestion, then withdrew to confer in private, and on
their return, so Badoglio's story runs, General Mason-Mac-
Farlane said that they had not drawn up the new document ;
but, acting under orders from their Governments, they were
presenting it for his signature. The cat was now out of the bag,
and the Governments as one would expect, were the villains
of the piece. After threats of ' the very gravest consequences '
if he did not sign, and hints by the American Generals (who
were obviously very much distressed) that the new armistice
might be brought into line with the armistice of September 3,
Marshal Badoglio, to save fresh suffering for Italy, and convinced of General Eisenhower's good faith, signed. He ends
his account of the meeting by saying that ' General Eisenhower kept his word '.

At the end of the meeting General Eisenhower handed the
Marshal a conciliatory letter stating that the new armistice
was supplementary to the military armistice of September 3 ;
that the terms were based on the situation prior to the cessation
of hostilities, that since then the situation had changed and
Italy had become a co-operator with the United Nations—
and much more in the same vein.

The ugly words Unconditional Surrender, however, continued to rankle in the mind of Marshal Badoglio. A few weeks
later he addressed a dignified letter to President Roosevelt and
Mr. Churchill, rehearsing all the circumstances and pointing

out that ' notwithstanding the passage from co-operation to belligerence and the assurances given me, the document which has been presented to me partially corrected, still contains the words Unconditional Surrender which did not appear in the original armistice '.

While these interminable delays, due largely to Unconditional Surrender were taking place, and while the Allied politicians were continuing to harass, by their meticulous insistence on a barren formula, the man who had risked his life in carrying out their own advice, the very man from whom they had most to expect, the Germans were pouring divisions into Italy and building up step by step the defence that caused such terrible losses to the Allies and such dreadful destruction to the fairest land in Europe. What had been called the ' soft ' underbelly was thus turned by Unconditional Surrender into fortified positions. The time lost was to cost us dear.

In addition, by that insistence, in the case of a country from which we had much to gain by kindness and consideration, we had given to Germany and Japan the clearest warning that in no circumstances would we listen to any terms that might be put forward short of the disastrous formula of Casablanca.

Germany and Unconditional Surrender

After the scurvy treatment of Marshal Badoglio and Italy it is not surprising that the Germans held out to the last possible moment. They intended to hold out longer still behind the mountain barriers of Bavaria, Austria, and North Italy, and General Eisenhower records that the object of this desperate expedient was to try and secure better terms than Unconditional Surrender. Fortunately the General foiled this plan, but the episode shows the desperation to which the phrase had driven our principal enemy. Apart from that, this unfortunate phrase prolonged the war for the German people to the last extremity of human endurance. Not one of the German leaders was willing to sign such humiliating terms as unconditional surrender, and few people in Britain or America know who did sign them. Their signatures will carry no more weight with posterity than did those of Mr. Hermann Mueller or Dr. Bell in the case of the Treaty of Versailles.

Japan and Unconditional Surrender

Japan held out with equal, if not greater tenacity. As late as July 21, 1945, long after the collapse of Germany, their principal ally, after the loss of almost all their war fleet and most of their mercantile marine, after much of their war potential and a large part of their capital had been destroyed by bombers, the Japanese Government, under the influence of the all-powerful military authorities sent their ambassador in Moscow, who greatly daring had insisted on the importance of immediate unconditional surrender, the following message:—

' We cannot consent to unconditional surrender under any circumstances. Even if the war drags on and more blood must be shed, we will fight as one man against the enemy in accordance with the Emperor's Command.' [1]

The Atomic Bomb

In these circumstances, to secure unconditional surrender without excessive prolongation of the war, the Leaders of the Western Allies decided at Potsdam in July, 1945, to resort to the ultimate expedient of the atomic bomb. It was a strange and risky decision. They knew that the bomb was the most cruel and deadly weapon that had ever been produced, and that its effects would fall indiscriminately on civilian and military targets. They knew that Japan had already approached Russia with a view to peace discussions. They knew that Russia was on the point of declaring war on Japan. Yet in this fatuous fight for a phrase, they would not pause to seek some more normal means of obtaining the terms they needed, nor would they wait to learn the effect of the Russian declaration of war.

There is no published evidence to show that they even inquired whether the use of the bomb was consistent with international law. Had they done so they would have found that, reduced to its simplest terms, the position was as follows:—

(i) The Washington Treaty of February 6, 1922, prohibits, among other things, ' the use in war of asphyxiating, poisonous, and other gases and all analogous *liquids, materials or devices* '.

---

[1] James F. Byrnes, *Speaking Frankly*, p. 211.

Since the atomic bomb would disperse great quantities of poisonous and lethal radio-activity, it obviously fell within the meaning of the words ' liquids, materials or devices '. The Washington Treaty, however, was never ratified because France could not accept other articles on submarine warfare, which formed part of the Treaty.

(ii) Nevertheless, the provisions of Article 5 of the Washington Treaty of 1922 were incorporated into the Geneva Convention, 1925, which extended them to include Bacteriological Warfare. Forty nations signed and ratified or adhered to the Geneva Protocol and between them it is binding. But the United States and Japan signed without ratifying or adhering, and neither of them was bound.

Mr. J. M. Spaight, in *The Atomic Problem. A new Approach*, which is the leading authority on this subject, sums up the position as follows:—

' The Treaty of Washington which forbade the use of gas never came into force. The Geneva Gas Protocol was never ratified by the United States. She was thus at liberty, under the letter of the law, to use gas bombs or, if atomic bombs were assimilated to them, such bombs also. Whether morally and ethically she was equally free to do so is a question which history will decide.'

Of two things, however, we may feel fairly certain, namely:—

(i) If the Allied Leaders had fallen into the hands of an enemy and had been tried as War Criminals the authors of the Charter would have made it their business to see that the use of the atomic bomb was declared to be a crime against international law.

(ii) If the enemy had solved the atomic problem and used the bomb first, its employment would have been included in the allied list of war crimes, and those who took the decision or who prepared and used the bomb, would have been condemned and hanged.

Expected Advantages

We are now in a position to discuss in the light of the past and of the actual results, how far the announcement of Unconditional Surrender was justified. But first it will be convenient

to sum up the advantages claimed for it by its authors ; these
were :

(1) A reasonable assurance of world peace through the destruction of German and Japanese war power ;

(2) The destruction of the philosophies in those countries based
on fear and hate;

(3) No vestige of the Nazi or Fascist power, no vestige of the
Japanese plotting machine will remain ;

(4) Punishment of the guilty and barbaric leaders ;

(5) The Allies will not be bound to the enemy at the moment
of surrender by any pact or obligation. Unconditional
surrender means that the victors will have a free hand ;

(6) No possibility of the Germans saying, as they did after the
last war, that they did not surrender, but only accepted
President Wilson's Fourteen Points. (As a matter of fact
they made many other excuses, *e.g.*, that they were not
beaten in battle, but starved by blockade, or that Hindenburg and Ludendorff lost their nerve).

None of these expected advantages materialized. The destruction of German and Japanese war power did not assure
world peace, because immediately after the end of the war the
Allies began to fall out, as so often happens, and the hopes of
world peace soon vanished. Such co-operation as had been
forced on us all by common adversity faded away when the risk
was removed. The Western Powers had saved Poland and
Roumania from the Nazis, as they had promised to do, but
only to hand them over with all Eastern Europe to the
Soviets whom these countries had always feared much more.
And soon the West found itself faced with a ' cold war ' waged
by communism, which threatened to become a hot war. If the
necessary destruction of Hitler had warded off a great danger,
the West had, by destroying German and Japanese war power,
and by alienating their populations, removed the barriers
against communism in Europe and the Far East and greatly
decreased the security of the whole world.

The destruction of philosophies, of hate and fear, mentioned
next in defence of the formula, has already received passing
comment on page 29. Christianity as a whole, the reformed
churches, the Jewish race and religion, Communism, Socialism
and many other 'isms, and their survival from the many attacks

upon them from inside and from outside, are perpetual witnesses to the impossibility of killing ideas, and philosophies and faiths by force. But, unless democracy can show greater unity and efficiency and more spirituality than is the case to-day, the philosophies of fear and hate will rear their ugly heads again. And we must not forget that Unconditional Surrender and War Crimes Trials are themselves part of a philosophy of hate that grew up without our noticing it during the war. It must be banned for ever.

Coming to Nazi and Fascist power and the Japanese plotting machine (point 3), most of us like to think that they have gone for ever. We thought on similar lines for a decade or more after World War I. But now all the world knows, what only a few realized in the nineteen twenties, that the foundations of German re-armament began to be laid immediately after the first war, under the noses of the Allied Commission on Disarmament, and that within fifteen years of the signature of the Treaty of Versailles Germany was about to become a menace to Western Europe. We must see that history does not repeat itself. It is too soon to say that these evils have vanished for ever.

Punishment of the guilty barbaric leaders (point 4) has been carried out. However, not only have all the political leaders but so many capable and experienced administrators and potential administrators been liquidated that the Governmental machines in ex-enemy countries are so weakened as to make their early economic recovery impossible. As Mr. Bevin put it in a statement quoted at the end of this Chapter, ' it left us without a single person with whom we could deal '.

It is true, owing to the announcement of Unconditional Surrender at the end of the war, the Allies found themselves bound to the enemy by no pact or obligation (point 5). As victors they had a free hand. But, this has not proved an advantage. It has merely enabled them to impose victor trials and other unwise things upon the enemy and to bring unpopularity upon them, and especially on this country in Germany. Moreover, although the Allies were not bound to their former enemies, neither were they bound to one another! The result is that they have no common ties, can never agree among themselves, and have made the very name of United Nations a by-word for disunion.

No doubt, there is much to criticize in the Peace Settlements —the undoubted *Diktats*—of 1919–20 ; but there is no question that the Western Allies in that war, by declaring their peace aims at the outset, by keeping them up to date throughout the war, and by their final overhaul after the armistice, and especially by avoiding the threat of Unconditional Surrender not only shortened the war but greatly facilitated the task of making a peace that at any rate lasted for twenty years.

There is very little to be said for the suggestion (point 6) that the imposition of Unconditional Surrender would prevent the Germans from saying that they did not surrender, as they said after World War I. For that story was proved false by the fact that it was the German Generals who first insisted on peace negotiations and by the humiliating terms of the armistice which they had to accept. When the right time comes the Germans will always find some false excuse to explain away their defeat. Some will say that Hitler was a maniac and misled them—and they will be able to support this view by quotations from Allied Leaders. Others will say that the Generals did not back them up. It was not wise to adopt Unconditional Surrender to forestall a return of the false German propaganda after the last war.

But, apart from the failure of Unconditional Surrender to realize the hopes of its authors—which were heavily criticized soon after its announcement—we shall see (in the next Chapter) that it also led to the trials of the war criminals, again lengthening and embittering the war, bleeding our country needlessly and making it impossible to conclude a real and lasting peace.

It has often been said that in any event we could not have made peace with Hitler or any of his gang. That is probably true. But in 1814 and 1815 we did not have to make peace with Napoleon, and in 1919 we did not have to make peace with the Kaiser, nor with the Crown Prince, nor their Generals. As we have seen earlier in this Chapter President Wilson made it quite clear almost on the eve of the armistice that we could not do that, and the alternative to acceptance by Germany of the Fourteen Points was surrender. In the second World War also, if we had not tied our hands by Unconditional Surrender and War Crimes Trials, it is quite possible that some opportunity might have been found for a corresponding procedure.

If we had not pulled the German nation together by giving them the courage of despair by these declarations, the Nazi régime might well have collapsed, whether from a General's *putsch* or otherwise. For example, after the surrender of Italy, or after the disaster in the Falaise pocket, or the failure of the winter offensive, or in the Ardennes, Hitler and his gang might have been glad enough to pull out as the Kaiser did in 1918, and to hand over to a German Badoglio to make peace. It is by no means impossible that even Russia might have been glad to call a halt to her staggering losses by the prospect of saving one, or two or three years of fearful war. Retreats and 'tactical variations' are consistent with Lenin's teaching.

Even Japan, with her tradition of refusal to surrender in any circumstances, might have been glad to save something from the wreck after the disaster in the Phillipines, if some face-saving pretence of negotiations had been open. There were Japanese statesmen of vision who desired peace. But she could not yet reconcile herself to the humiliation of Unconditional Surrender.

All this shows how slight, and how hard of realization are the benefits, and especially how grave may be the consequences of a threat of Unconditional Surrender before or during a war. It leads to trickery and chicanery with its climax, extreme cruelty, carnage and destruction in the case of a besieged city like Carthage ; to a legacy of bitterness, as in South Africa ; to endangering the conclusion of an armistice, as in World War I, or to its cancellation as in Aetolia in 191 B.C. ; to trickery and chicanery, once more, resulting in exasperation, discouragement and reduced co-operation of a potential ally, as in Italy in World War II ; to extremes of suffering, intensified brutality and retaliation as in Germany ; and the culminating tragedy of the two Atomic Bombs in Japan. It is indeed a sorry story with little or nothing to set on the other side.

And after the war, in Germany at any rate, the result was to make the conclusion of peace and the rehabilitation of the country impossible. To quote Mr. Bevin's words in the House of Commons on 21 July, 1949:—

" I must go back for a moment to the declaration of Unconditional Surrender made at Casablanca, on which neither the British Cabinet nor any other Cabinet had a chance to say a word. It was in the middle of a war and it was just made.

But it left us with a Germany without law, without a constitution, without a single person with whom we could deal, without a single institution to grapple with the situation, and we have had to build from the bottom with nothing at all. . . ." [1]

Mr. Churchill disagreed as to these after-effects, but in this matter Mr. Bevin was bearing the burden and the responsibility, and his word must prevail.

The only nation that gained any advantage from the Unconditional Surrender policy was Russia, who, owing to the lengthening of the war was able to over-run Eastern Europe and impose her own political system therein. This was facilitated by the fact that she had the wisdom to avoid the imposition on those countries of Unconditional Surrender.

[1] *Hansard*, Commons, Col. 1593. Author's italics. In a further statement in the House of Commons on 17 November 1949, Mr. Winston Churchill corrected his earlier account. After consulting official papers he had found that in fact he had consulted the Cabinet. After reading the messages that had passed he continued—" It will be seen that the opinion of the Cabinet was not against the policy of unconditional surrender. They only disapproved of it not being applied to Italy as well. . . . I have the strong feeling that I thought that that would influence the President, too. This is borne out by the agreed communiqué which was drafted by the Combined Chiefs of Staff and approved by both of us, and which contains no mention of unconditional surrender . . ." (Hansard, Commons, 17 November 1949, Cols. 2224–2225). This statement clears Mr. Churchill of the charge of not consulting the Cabinet, and tends to confirm that he was not very enthusiastic about the policy, especially if Italy was to be included in its scope. It does not throw much light on the wisdom or otherwise of unconditional surrender nor on its subsequent consequences.

CHAPTER THREE

THE GERMAN TRIALS

How did this policy of first enforcing Unconditional Surrender and next putting on Trial the leaders of the defeated nations work out in detail? I had opposed this policy at the time, particularly in my speeches in the House of Lords after I had left the Churchill Administration. Perhaps I can do no better than to recall, in its proper setting, my speech on the German War Crimes Trials (of May 5, 1949). It was beset with many of the inconveniences of all parliamentary Debates. The Notices and Orders of the Day contained a long list of Government business that had precedence over our debate, including two or three rather ' sticky ' Bills. Additional delay was caused by the interruption of the debate on one of these Bills by the interpolation of a statement on the Four Power Agreement on Germany, on which the Party Leaders had to make some comments before the normal business could be resumed. The Bill itself, after a mildly acrimonious discussion, which did not improve the parliamentary atmosphere, involved a division which always takes some time.

All such business however is important, and the House of Lords contains such a variety of expert knowledge that even what appears to the outsider minor business will very often produce a well informed and interesting debate as well as amendments to Bills of great importance to the country. So we ' sat in the pavilion ' for some hours and it was 5.30 p.m. before the Bishop of Chichester took the floor with a splendid speech introducing his Motion against continued War Crimes Trials. He was followed by Lord Henderson, the Parliamentary Under-Secretary for Foreign Affairs, and Viscount Simon, and it was past 6.30 p.m. before I was called. As there were several important speakers to follow me, and the House wanted to hear the Lord Chancellor's reply, I had to cut down my carefully prepared speech from my estimate of forty minutes to twenty-three minutes—always a difficult process at short notice.[1] The largest share of the cuts had to fall on a careful examination I had made of the Nuremberg Tribunal's narrative of the German side of the Norway campaign, which was to have been a key feature in my speech : it is in Chapter Four.

I rose at 6.33 p.m. and said : " I came here to-day to support to the full the Motion of the right reverend Prelate. When the statement was made from the Government Bench, I hoped at first that it was going to give the right reverend Prelate considerable satisfaction, but I am sorry to say I am very disappointed now. Apart from the trial of Von Manstein, there seem to be trials still going on all over Germany. I entirely agree with what my noble and learned friend Viscount Simon has just said, that these trials ought to be stopped and that His Majesty's Government ought to set the example in the matter. Still, I congratulate the Government on having made some advance in that direction, and I hope that when I raise the question of Japanese trials a fortnight hence I shall find a greater advance.

The Origin of the Trials

" To appreciate the position, I think we have to review it rather broadly. These trials began with the Nuremberg trials; they are really all offshoots in one way or another. Nuremberg was born in a bad year, 1943 ; a policy of virulent threats was adopted in 1943 and has bedevilled the world ever since. That policy, in which so far as I am aware, no Commander-in-Chief, or Chief of Staff had any concern, was inaugurated by the announcement by President Roosevelt and Mr. Churchill, but not by Mr. Stalin, who was not present, of ' Unconditional Surrender ' at Casablanca on January 20, 1943.

The Wider Policy and its Effects

" That was a great gift to Goebbels's propaganda, rallied the disillusioned German people to Hitler, strengthened the

[1] Owing to the unavoidable curtailment of the debate on May 5, some of the comments on my speech were only made during the debate on the Tokyo War Crimes Trials on May 19. My replies to these are included in the present Chapter, which will explain why occasionally I have inserted in brackets the words ' on May 19, 1949 ', to avoid mixing up the two subjects more than can be helped. Verbatim extracts are from the Parliamentary Debates, House of Lord's Official Report, and are reproduced with the permission of the Controller of H.M. Stationery Office.

resistance of the enemy and greatly prolonged the war by making it impossible for the Allies to offer peace on less humiliating terms in either the West or the Far East. Then, on November 1, nine months later, came the announcement from Moscow of the intention of the Allies to punish the Nazi leaders. That threat, like all threats, stimulated retaliation and again postponed peace *sine die*, because it threatened everybody who could make peace ; they were told that they were all to be killed or imprisoned. Even to-day we have no German Treaty. Moreover, as a result of the bitterness engendered, the war became a fight to a finish and, through no fault of the Allied Service chiefs, degenerated into a sadistic orgy of competitive frightfulness—V1 and V2 weapons, U-boat warfare and frantic war crimes on one side, and, on the other, unlimited bombing, culminating in the crowning catastrophe of the atomic bomb.

" I think history will attribute to this ganglion of desperate policies the following consequences : first, the prolongation of the war to a point where we were bled white while Russia was extending her grip over all Eastern Europe and accomplishing Stalin's published aims ; secondly, the failure to make peace with Germany for four years or more after the end of hostilities ; thirdly, the replacement of German tyranny by Russian despotism, the estrangement from the Western Allies of Germany and Russia, the disappearance of the historic frontiers between Eastern and Western Europe and of the balance of power for their defence ; and fourthly, a legacy of bitterness, confusion and hatred which stifled the United Nations from its birth and still continues."

It is interesting to recall that in winding up the debate for the Government the Lord Chancellor charged me with irrelevance. That is a view that I cannot accept ; each of my readers can judge for himself as he peruses the speech. The main objects of the Bishop of Chichester, whose motion I was supporting, were far reaching—an immediate amnesty, no more prosecutions, no more surrender to foreign Governments and a reconsideration of all sentences passed. How could those aims be better backed than by showing, as I attempted to do, that from beginning to end these trials had brought misery to mankind ; that they had originated in a policy of hate, that they had embittered and prolonged the war, promoted the obnoxious policies of the Soviet Union while bringing us to exhaustion, made the conclusion of peace impossible and established profoundly dangerous precedents for the future. Moreover, if I erred, it was in good company, for the Bishop also reviewed the past and often arrived at conclusions very similar to my own.

Effects of the Trials

I continued : " So much for the wider policy and its results, in which the trials of war criminals had, and unfortunately still have their place. Of the trials themselves it can already be said that, besides starting new trials all over Germany, they have been imitated all over Europe, resulting in the judicial persecution and often death of countless and often innocent people—kings, statesmen, cardinals, politicians, generals, diplomats and I know not whom. And that again will continue until the German and Japanese trials are brought to an end. Secondly, it can be said that a deplorable precedent has been set for future wars. At both Nuremberg and Tokio, as the right reverend Prelate has said, the victors tried and judged the vanquished. The tribunals were established by and derived their powers from the victors alone, for the trial of the vanquished and of no one else. It was by the victors alone that the Charter and the Code of International Law were drawn up. There was something cynical . . . in the spectacle of British, French and American judges sitting on the Bench with colleagues who, however impeccable as individuals, represented a country which before, during and since the trials has perpetrated half the political crimes in the calendar. And in spite of the specious arguments (on page 38) of the Nuremberg Judgement, I do not see how anyone can deny that under a cloak of justice these trials were just the old, old story—one law for the victors and another for the vanquished. *Vae victis* ! "

The reference to the position of the judges representing Great Britain, France and America sitting with the judge of the Soviet Union, a country suspected of many of the crimes of which the prisoners were accused, was of course not intended as a reflection on the judges themselves, but on political errors that placed them in such a position. The crimes to which I referred were not, as Lord Oaksey seems to have assumed, the blockade of Berlin, if that was a crime, which I doubt, but such matters as the Soviet aggressions against Eastern Poland (September, 1939) Finland (November, 1939), and the three Baltic States (annexed in the summer of 1940), as well as the seizure at the end of the war of political control and the suppression of liberty in the European countries east of the Iron Curtain. To those may be added the list mentioned by the Bishop of Chichester in the following passage : ' First the Charter deals only with the crimes of the vanquished ; but it is very difficult for a defeated foe to appreciate the justice of punishing such crimes as the *deportation of civilian populations in occupied territory, looting, murder of prisoners of war, and devastation not justified by military necessity*,[1] when similar charges could be brought against one or more of the Allies, but are not brought.'

Dr. Bell, however, pitched it rather low in suggesting that the difficulty of appreciating the justice of such punishments is confined to a defeated foe. The same difficulty is felt to-day by many in the victor countries too, and is among the main causes of the widespread misgivings felt about the policy of these trials in Great Britain and America.

' The making of the Charter ', declared the Nuremberg Tribunal, ' was the exercise of the sovereign legislative power by the countries to which the German Reich unconditionally surrendered ; and the undoubted right of those countries to legislate for the occupied territories has been recognized by the civilized world '. But the trouble is that many thinking citizens of the civilized world, in this country as in America, France and other countries, have grave doubts, first as to whether the victor countries really had these rights, and second as to whether they were wise to exercise them in that manner. Those doubts have been augmented by the United Nations Declaration of Human Rights in December, 1948 (see Chapter VIII).

Lord Justice Wright (in a moderate and persuasive speech on May 19, 1949) held that the only questions were: ' Did the man have a fair trial ? Were the facts put before the court ? And

[1] Author's italics.

did the court impartially come to the best view it could ? '
Even those questions, however, raise grave doubts. All the
world has paid its tribute to the fair and masterly conduct of the
trial by Lord Oaksey.   But, even so, can anyone claim that
an optimum standard of justice can be obtained in any international court, with judges from nations whose ideas on justice
differ fundamentally, in some of which the judiciary are part
of the Governmental machinery ; and where a score or more
of prisoners have to be tried at once—to say nothing of difficulties of language, interpretation, gathering political and other
information and so forth ?   Yet, everyone with us must agree
that nothing short of an optimum standard of justice is admis-
sible where men's lives and liberties, and the reputation of great
nations before history, are at stake.   Even the dissenting opinion
of the Soviet Member of the Nuremberg Tribunal against the
acquittal of Schacht, von Papen and Fritsche, and against the
sentence on Hess of life imprisonment instead of death, gives
food for serious thought.

In any event, it is difficult to believe that the trials, however
fair in fact, will be accepted as such by the present generation
of the vanquished. In fact, we know that they are not.   Still
less are they likely to be accepted by posterity as fair.   And if
they are not, then they will rankle for centuries in men's hearts
even if they are on a different plane from the burning of Jeanne
d'Arc, condemned as a witch by the Bishop of Beauvais' Tribunal, burned in the market place of Rouen in May, 1431,
and canonised as a saint a few years ago.

Those are some of the thoughts that should have been in the
minds of those who devised this policy.   The sooner we can
bring the trials to an end the better.   And the franker we are
in admitting our mistakes to ourselves and to the world at large
the sooner shall we be able to settle terms of peace and restore
harmony among the nations.

The Precedent for the Future

That brings me to my remarks on the danger of the War
Crimes Trials as a political precedent, which no one attempted
to answer.   " To grasp the political danger of the precedent, let
us imagine that the countries of Eastern Europe have over-run
many of the countries of Europe. Can you imagine that they

would not follow the Nuremberg precedent faithfully, writing their own charter, defining and creating their own ' international ' laws and establishing their own tribunals ? The employment of the atomic bomb would be decreed as a breach of the laws of war— which is an arguable proposition—and everyone they could lay hands on, who had ever been concerned in its use in any war, would be tried and hanged. The Atlantic Pact has already been denounced by Russia and her satellites as a breach of international law, and those who have aided and abetted it and been concerned in its military planning would be advised not to fall into Russian hands. From Sir Alexander Cadogan's remarks at the United Nations a day or two ago, we know how their trials are conducted:

' The official view of the administration of justice in these countries is that it should not be impartial, but must serve the ends of the régime in power. One of the few certain things we know about the trial of Cardinal Mindszenty is that the judge was not independent because he was told what verdict he was expected to give, and knew that his job depended upon his giving it '.[1]

The Military Precedent

" Another dangerous precedent created by this trial is in connection with defensive planning. There are, or will be, defensive planners with the United Nations, regional organizations like the Atlantic Pact, or individual nations. Upon the discipline and loyalty of the planners, whether military or civilian, to the supreme control of their respective Governments the whole safety of the nation or of any group of nations will depend. But those primitive virtues of discipline and loyalty seem to have been forgotten by the pedants who devised Article 8 of the Charter. This lays down that : ' . . . the fact that a defendant acted pursuant to an order of his Government or of a superior shall not free him from responsibility.' That confronts the individual planner with an impossible dilemma between duty and conscience. Shall he obey the order, or shall he seek the shelter of some international law—as it will be interpreted, not

[1] At this point five lines containing a facetious speculation as to what the judges would say, if they could speak freely, is omitted because Lord Oaksey protested against it, and I agree that it was ill-timed.

necessarily by his own fellow countrymen, not necessarily by
the Nuremberg Charter (which we are told was so good), but
by the Victor in the war, who may be his enemy, with a totally
different ethical standard? It is just placing a premium on
cowardice and escapism in the proper carrying out of orders."

In this connection it may be noted that the Bishop of Chichester recalled how, " Field-Marshal Viscount Montgomery in
Paris, at the Franco-British luncheon on July 8 of last year,
said that the Nuremberg trials made the waging of unsuccessful
war a crime, for the Generals of the defeated side would be tried
and then hanged." Admiral of the Fleet the Earl of Cork and
Orrery who spoke immediately after me, also remarked on this
aspect, which troubles the Fighting Services considerably. The
matter, however, concerns not only the Fighting Services but
also Civil Servants of all kinds—Foreign Office Officials and
Ambassadors, Representatives of Departments concerned in
Finance, Trade and Shipping, Scientists or persons engaged
in any ancillary to military planning. Ministers especially are
liable to be held responsible for their decisions. No official
answer was given to those who mentioned this aspect. Instead
the Government spokesman limited himself to the Tribunal's
attitude towards the law. This, however, cannot set these
doubts at rest. The precedent has been established.

The rôle played by this planning precedent is also illustrated
by the operations prepared for the invasion of Norway. Hastily
condensing my exposition owing to the limited time that was
left to me, I said : " Contrary to general belief, the history on
which the Nuremberg judgements and findings were based is
not accurate. I have made a careful comparison between the
invasion of Norway, as described in the judgements, and the
description of it in Mr. Churchill's memoirs *The Gathering
Storm*. Of course, those memoirs were not published at the
time, but that evidence was available if the tribunal had thought
it worth while to get it, but their judgement was based entirely
upon the evidence that they obtained from the Germans. They
did not find out what was going on in the Allied countries. I
will just mention one or two points. Had the judges called for

that evidence, they would have discovered that the planning of the aggression first began in this country. It was on September 29, 1939, four days before Admiral Raeder's memorandum, which is always quoted as being the first step in German planning, that Mr. Churchill called for plans here.[1] That was the start of the plans for what was eventually carried out, the mining of the Norwegian Leads, which Mr. Churchill described a little later on as ranking as ' a major operation of war '. He then discussed the probability that, if it was carried out, Germany would spread the war to Norway and Sweden, which he thought would be to our advantage ; and towards the end he put in a plea for anticipating them, even though it meant a violation of neutrality. Those are all just the things that the Germans were doing and thinking about, *mutatis mutandis*.

" Then the judges would have had their memory recalled to the *Altmark* incident, which was actually the first breach of international law, apart from the sinkings of neutral ships. The Norwegians protested violently against this as a breach of international law and, as Mr. Churchill comments, it no doubt gave the Germans ' a spur to action '. All those things were overlooked by the judges because they took no evidence from the other side. In my opinion, the result is that their summing-up is quite incorrect namely that ' in the light of all the available evidence, it is impossible to accept the contention that the invasions of Denmark and Norway were defensive, and in the opinion of the Tribunal they were acts of aggressive war '. The very important operation of the mining of the Norwegian Leads actually took place on April 8 and was criticized by the Norwegians. German retaliation was just coming ; but, all the same, they protested against it, and the Germans came in the next day—April 9. So both in the planning and in the execution, we were beforehand. I think that was a very good thing. I think it showed great foresight on Mr. Churchill's part. But we did actually begin the planning and we actually committed the first aggression, though by a very short head. If the judges had obtained that evidence, the judgements would have been different."

[1] I have since discovered an earlier Memorandum still. Also written by Mr. Churchill, it is dated September 19, that is fourteen days before Raeder's. I return to it on p. 72.

I was given a fleeting opportunity to elucidate the matter a little further during the Debate on the Tokyo trials on May 19, when the Earl of Perth reopened the question of the aggression on Norway and asked me a direct question. Again I was speaking *ex tempore* and without notes and my remarks had to be brief, as they were an interruption of Lord Perth's speech. I said : " May I answer that straight away ? It raises the very large question of what is aggression. The British plan was to cut the Norwegian Leads, as Mr. Churchill made quite clear in the memoranda which he had published in *The Gathering Storm*. That operation, the operation of cutting the German Leads, was a major operation of war—and Mr. Churchill explained it—because it cut off completely the German main supply of material for steel. Mr. Churchill said if we could do that, we should bring them very low indeed by reason of their shortage of steel, and their munitions industry would be crippled. That is what you might call a throttling operation. What the Germans said was : ' We cannot afford to allow this, but we cannot stop it except by an operation on the coast line '. They had no sea power and no aerodromes in the area. There was no way in which they could deal with that menace except by occupying the country. So while we were prepared to throttle them, they were prepared to invade and occupy Norway. I would point out to your Lordships that this is where the question becomes so difficult. Is it not just as bad to throttle a man as to stab him ? I think if our operation was non-aggressive, theirs, which they took as the only way they could save themselves from being throttled, was equally non-aggressive. I was a member of the Cabinet at that time of the war, and we had no illusions about the matter. Everyone knew that the Germans had to do it. As I say, it is all in the memoranda published by Mr. Churchill. So my answer is quite definite that the two operations are both major operations of war, within limitations, and they are inseparable. I believe that that would be the military view."

One more opportunity arose, at the end of the Debate on May 19, to make a brief reference to Norway when I was able to bring out one point that no one had mentioned. The Germans had, at the very outset of the war given the Norwegian Government warning, that, if they allowed their neutrality to be violated by any other country, the Germans would consider themselves free to defend their interests : " On September 2, before we were in the war, the Germans told the Norwegians that they were going to respect their neutrality. But in telling them that, they warned the Norwegians most seriously that if anyone else violated that neutrality, they would hold themselves free to take necessary measures. So when we did commit what I agree was a minor breach of Norwegian neutrality on February 16, the Germans naturally backed up that view, and on February 20 Hitler told the General in command to get on with it. On March 1, the German Fuehrer decided to go in. They had a very good excuse when the Norwegians protested against our mining those fjords. Norway was very important to us both, and of enormous value defensively, as well as offensively. We wanted to cut the line, and the Germans wanted to prevent the steel line being cut."

The Tribunal's Evidence

Before leaving the subject of Norway, it is necessary to mention that the President of the Nuremberg Court, Lord Oaksey, resented my suggestion that the Tribunal's judgement was based entirely upon the evidence obtained from the Germans and that they did not find out what was going on in allied countries. He claimed that any evidence that was remotely relevant, and which was applied for by the defence, was obtained. Witnesses were brought from all over Europe, interrogatories were sent to America and to England and counsel for the defence were even allowed to search naval files at the Admiralty in London.

The extraordinary thing, however, is that the results of all this activity, so far as Norway is concerned, is ignored in the part of the Judgement dealing with it. (Cmd. 6964/46, pp. 27–30). We hear all about Hitler, Doenitz, Keitel, Jodl, Raeder, Rosenberg and others—all, that is to say that tells against them—but there is not a ray of light on what the British War Cabinet, the Chief's of Staff Committee, Mr. Churchill and the British Naval Staff were doing. Are we intended to believe that in this vitally important theatre of operations our powerful organization for war control was doing no planning ? Did it not occur to this International *Military* Tribunal to find out whether there was anything in the way of allied military planning and execution which might have explained, mitigated the act or even justified the German planning and execution ? Except for a brief reference (at the bottom of page 29) to some British documents captured by the Germans, there is no hint in the Judgement of any planning at all on the Allied side. Or were no questions asked since they might lead to the kind of awkward—politically awkward—queries so rightly feared in 1945 by Mr. Justice Jackson ? So puzzled was I that I decided to make an official test. I put down on the Order Paper of the House of Lords a question. That was on May 24. And this is the result as shown in the Lords *Official Report* of June 23, 1949 :

LORD HANKEY asked His Majesty's Government whether the following documents published in Mr. Churchill's book *The Second World War*, Volume I (" The Gathering Storm ") were communicated to the Nuremberg Tribunal :

September 19, 1939 :
First Lord to First Sea Lord and others. Pages 421–2.

September 29, 1939 :
Memo, by First Lord of Admiralty for War Cabinet, Norway and Sweden. Pages 422–3.

September 29, 1939 :
First Lord to the Assistant Chief of Naval Staff. Pages 423–4.

December 16, 1939 :
Norway—Iron-Ore Traffic. Note by the First Lord of the Admiralty. Pages 430–439.

THE PARLIAMENTARY UNDER-SECRETARY OF STATE FOR FOREIGN AFFAIRS (LORD HENDERSON): No trace can be found of the four documents in question having been communicated to the Nuremberg Tribunal.

Now the Norwegian question is merely one amongst the innumerable highly important matters with which Mr. Churchill deals in his books. Yet, even so he has, as by chance, produced essential evidence which the Nuremberg Tribunal did not succeed in collecting, either because its system was inadequate or conceivably because the papers were not applied for by the defence. But how could the defence know of or even guess the

existence of these secret papers ? It is important because it is
evidence which shatters one of the charges brought against
the German leaders on which they were found guilty.

A Challenge to the Tribunal's History

My comments on the Nuremberg Judgement's account of
the Nowegian campaign, condensed and mutilated though
they were, had constituted an appreciable indictment of the
Tribunal's history. I next developed this thesis in a wider
field :

" But, if the tribunal's account of the Norway campaign is
wrong history, that is equally true of the even more important
introductory review of the rise of Hitler and his gang with which
the Judgement opens for the purpose of showing the background
of the aggressive war and the war crimes charged in the indictment. That is a serious statement to make. It is true that there
are very few errors of commission. It is a perfectly correct
account, if you look through it. But the sins of omission—they
really make one's hair stand on end ! Here is a great historical
account of the fall of a nation to an abominable system and
leader, and there is hardly a single word on what was the provocation. It is true that they do just mention one point—
namely, Hitler's aim of removing ' the disgrace of Versailles '.
That appealed naturally to the German people, as have all
appeals for freedom. But not a word appears of such provocations as the occupation of the Ruhr in 1923 which, rightly
or wrongly, was denounced at the time by the leaders of every
British Party and in every Dominion as a flagrant aggression.
There was not one word of the use of Black troops in the
Rhineland garrison, which was very irritating to the Germans ; nor of the attempts to detach Bavaria and Saxony from
Germany ; nor of the endless pinpricks over reparations up
to 1932.

" There is another great cause of the Second Great War
which is not even mentioned—namely, the failure of the
Allies who had both the right under the Treaty and the force,
though they lacked the will, to stop German rearmament.
Mr. Churchill mentions that point at the very beginning of his

Gathering Storm in this caption : ' Theme of the volume : How the English-speaking peoples through their unwisdom, carelessness and good nature, allowed the wicked to rearm '.

"It was not only the English people ; it was others too. But by slackness and by such things as the British Ten-years rule, they did allow the Germans to rearm. The Allies were gradually reduced to such a state of moral and physical disarmament that in the thirties they had neither the will nor the power to halt the Germans. Those are some of the major causes of the war. It will be said, in the 'twenties the Allies goaded the Germans beyond endurance, and in the 'thirties they did not stop them as they ought to have done ; the feeble protests that were made were almost a condoning of German aggression."

This challenge to the Tribunal's history was criticized both by Lord Oaksey and the Earl of Perth. The former pointed out that ' the tribunal had some years to cover in their judgement, and though they recited the rise of Hitler to power they could scarcely be expected to write a complete history of the period '.

The object of the historical review is described on page 3 of the Judgement as follows :

' For the purpose of showing the background of the aggressive war and war crimes charged in the Indictment, the Tribunal will begin by reviewing some of the events that followed the first world war, and in particular, by tracing the growth of the Nazi Party under Hitler's leadership to a position of supreme power from which it controlled the destiny of the whole German people, and *paved the way for the alleged commission of all the crimes charged against the defendants.*'[1]

My point is that in a historical summary of events which paved the way to the political crimes with which the Germans were charged, any extenuating circumstances and any evidence of provocation tending to show what induced the Germans to accept Hitler and his gang as masters of their fate ought to have been included. The particular examples of provocation which I quoted, and which were queried by my old friend the Earl of Perth, were the Occupation of the Ruhr, the use of black troops in the Rhineland, and the attempts to detach certain parts of Germany from the Reich. I had thought this

[1] Author's italics.

was common knowledge. Standard historical works certainly have come to the same conclusion ; H. A. L. Fisher, for instance writes in his *History of Europe* (Vol. III) :

' The representative of the retributive spirit in France was Poincaré, a blunt, solid, very able and industrious lawyer, and of all the political figures on the French stage during the crisis of the war and afterwards the most commanding. The idea that the exchange of a militarist Empire for a Socialist republic denoted an improvement of the German heart, or the British argument that the the whole continent would suffer from the ruin of Germany, did not impress this stern lawyer from Lorraine. He wanted reparations and security—reparations at once, security always—and since he did not believe in the German protestations of poverty, but thought that the Germans were fraudulent debtors, seeking by every dishonest ruse to evade their liabilities, he was resolved that they should feel the full weight of a military occupation. So, *to the burning indignation of the Germans, black colonial troops were quartered in the Rhineland towns, and when even thus deliveries were backward, Poincaré marched an army into the Ruhr.*[1]

The occupation of the Ruhr, *against which every British party protested*, was one of those extreme historical misfortunes which, when suffering has reached an intolerable point, supply their own correction. . . .' (p. 1198).

The same conclusion was reached in *Europe in the Nineteenth and Twentieth Centuries*, by Grant and Temperley :

' To suffering was added the sting of injustice. The French occupation of the Ruhr caused Germany deep humiliation. Great Britain finally avowed it was illegal and admitted it to be contrary to the Versailles Treaty.' (p. 619).

Mr. Winston Churchill, in *The Second World War*, Vol. II, page 10, is as insistent as anyone. He refers to Poincaré's attempts to make an independent Rhineland under French aegis; to the strong British and American condemnation of the French occupation of the Ruhr, to the rage aroused in Germany, and the terrible financial reactions, and to the sufferings and bitterness, which marched together.

The Earl of Perth suggested that the memories of the occupation of the Ruhr, etc., were obliterated by the Treaty of Locarno

[1] Author's italics.

and the entry of Germany into the League of Nations ; but the historians do not support that thesis :

' In 1925 the Pact of Locarno gave a chance to the moderates, and inaugurated an era of appeasement and of hope. But Reparations, with its attendant evils of unemployment, of hunger, of inflation, and of taxation, pressed ever more heavily upon the people. . . . The above sketch gives an outline of Germany's troubles, but it makes no attempt to estimate her real anguish and suffering. Hunger, humiliation, hopelessness for the future, the prospect of eternal poverty and eternal disgrace, the reduction of Germany to the rank of a minor power, the restriction of her army to one hundred thousand men, the constant interference from outside, the hopeless inferiority to which she saw herself condemned, these were permanent features in Germany's life in the decade after the war. The rays of hope which broke in upon her from time to time lasted only for a moment and left her to a more enduring despair . . . They drifted gradually into a curious condition in which they were ready to surrender everything into the hands of an individual . . . .' (Grant and Temperley, pp. 619–620).

Those passages show how in the 'twenties the mistaken policy of some of the nations of Western Europe reduced the Germans to a state of dejection and misery in which they succumbed readily to Hitler's promises and message of hope and recovery. Hitler, however, could not have sustained himself for long unless the Western Powers, this time largely under British precept and example, had not by physical and moral disarmament lost the power and the will to exercise their rights under the Treaties of Peace. A record of the growth of the Nazi Party under Hitler's leadership to a position of supreme power, which makes no mention of these all-important external factors, can hardly be described as fair or just. It certainly is not history. Yet, by staging legal trials was it not expected of lawyers to turn historians ?

The conclusion I was forced to draw was this :

" I am always told that all the convicted persons were judged and convicted of war crimes, as well as of political crimes, and that the sentences imposed were not affected by the judgements on crimes against peace. That is a most unsatisfactory answer, because to my mind it is clear that before history a cardinal error has been committed in indicting a whole nation of political crimes, without including any extenuating circumstances such as those I have mentioned. I do not confess to any great affection for the Germans but I admit that I am very jealous of our reputation for fairness, and I am horrified at the idea of future Anglo-German relations being poisoned by false history, which will also give the Germans an excuse for making martyrs of Hitler and his gang. These defects were due to two causes. One was that the tribunal never took any evidence of what was being done by other countries ; and secondly, that at the time they had no expert assessors with them.

"Summing up, I cannot see that we gained anything by the Nuremberg trials, and I shall seek to show (in a fortnight's time) that we have gained nothing from the Tokyo trials. Therefore, I most cordially support the right reverend Bishop's proposals. (*i.e.*, to drop this policy). The most urgent thing is to bring all these trials to an end, and if other nations will not agree, to decline any further British co-operation. We must not be too mealy-mouthed about it. It is four years after the war. As I said on February 18, 1948, from this Box : ' As a first step, trials and prosecutions of war criminals should be dropped and there should be a universal amnesty. "Vengeance is mine, and I will repay," saith the Lord. Let us leave it at that. It is not by fear and threats that the world can be won to decency and kindness, but by charity '."

CHAPTER FOUR

NORWAY

A MORE detailed scrutiny of the Norwegian campaign repays study, throwing light as it does on the problem of aggression and of the trial of national leaders. Politics, Trials and Errors stand out in bold relief.

The strategical situation in 1939 was very similar to the position in 1807 as described by Mahan (if we substitute 'Hitler' for 'Napoleon'): 'England had no army wherewith to meet Hitler ; Hitler had no Navy to cope with that of his enemy. As in the case of an impregnable fortress, the only alternative for either of these contestants was to reduce the other by starvation. On the common frontier, the coast line, they met in a deadly strife in which no weapon was drawn.'[1]

In the fortress of Europe no section of the whole perimeter was more important in 1939 than the coast of Norway, for in winter, when the Baltic was apt to freeze, there was an uninterrupted channel of sheltered neutral waters from Narvik to the Skagerrak through which German ships could bring to Germany the produce of the Swedish Gällivare iron ore mines, which were of vital importance to the German steel industry. In the whole of the vast naval theatre of war there was no offensive operation open to Britain from which so much advantage could be gained as the cutting of this life-line of German communications. In the same way, there was no more important defensive operation for Germany than to safeguard this key traffic against interruption. So long as Norwegian neutrality could be preserved the route was secure, and by that means it had been kept open throughout the First World War. Norwegian neutrality was therefore the first aim of the Germans. Obviously this was the reason why as early as September 2, as mentioned in the Nuremberg Judgement, the Germans promised ' to respect the territory of the Norwegian State ' but at the same time gave warning that they expected, 'on its side

---

[1] Mahan, *Influence of Sea Power upon the French Revolution and Empire,* chap. xviii.

that Norway will observe an unimpeachable neutrality towards
the Reich and will not tolerate any breaches of Norwegian
neutrality by any third party . . . ' Further, the Norwegians
were warned that if any such breach of neutrality did occur
' the Reich Government would then obviously be compelled to
safeguard the interests of the Reich in such way as the resulting
situation might dictate '. That was a useful piece of prevision
for the Germans as events turned out, but although it is mentioned in the Judgement it is only used as evidence of German
bad faith.

If, however, their plans for securing neutrality should fail
and Great Britain should mine the Norwegian Leads, the Germans could have no way of protecting their life-line for the
transport of the Gällivare ore except by occupying the Norwegian Coast, since their fleet was small and they had no aero-
drome in that part of the world. For Germany the occupation
of Norway, besides its defensive importance for the protection
of the Gällivare iron ore, would of course have, in addition,
the offensive advantage of facilitating their operations by U-
Boat and aircraft against Britain and her sea communications.
Conversely, for Britain it was important defensively to exclude
the Germans as long as possible from obtaining those offensive
advantages.

For both nations, therefore, an operation in Norway had the
greatest interest, both defensively and offensively. In the case
of Great Britain the prospect was a strangling operation, namely
the mining of the Leads, which was planned very early in the
war ; it was always recognized however, that some troops
would be required in addition to protect bases and aerodromes.
In the case of Germany, the projected operation whether considered from a defensive or offensive point of view, necessarily
had to take the form of a military occupation.

The Nuremberg Tribunal, which by the way never adopted
any definition of what constituted an aggression, pronounced
the German invasion of Norway an act of aggressive warfare.
Several of the accused who took part in the planning were found
guilty of planning, preparing, initiating or waging aggressive
war in Norway. They were condemned on that count. But
the Tribunal never so much as mentioned the British strangling
operation, which, as we shall see, actually preceded the German

operation at the stages both of planning and execution, and did not say whether this too was an act of aggression or not.

Such an omission is the more curious because events in the World War, 1914–18, had brought the problems of Norway prominently to light. In August, 1918, when an anti-submarine mine barrage had been laid right across the North Sea, it was felt by the British War Cabinet to be intolerable that German U-Boats and surface ships should be able to evade the mines by using the Norwegian Leads. The Norwegian Government were pressed to lay mines themselves to defend their neutrality, but declined to do so. The objections to mining the waterways, ourselves, however, were found to be too great. To quote the *Official History* :

' At a Conference held on board the *Queen Elizabeth* at the end of August, the Commander-in-Chief (Lord Beatty) said it would be most repugnant to the officers and men in the Grand Fleet to steam in overwhelming strength into the waters of a small but high-spirited people and coerce them. If the Norwegians resisted, as they probably would, blood would be shed ; this, said the Commander-in-Chief, " would constitute a crime as bad as any that the Germans had committed elsewhere ".[1] The Tribunal's version of the story will now be tested further by following events step by step.

At the Planning Stage

The Tribunal (page 27) says that the idea of attacking Norway originated with Raeder and Rosenberg, and in support of this statement of fact they refer to various Memoranda by the former dated October 3, 6, and 10, 1939. They mention also that in October and November, 1939, Raeder and Rosenberg were working on the occupation of Norway. That, they say, was the beginning of German planning.

But the Judgement does not mention that in a Minute dated September 19, 1939, Mr. Winston Churchill, First Lord of the British Admiralty, after consulting the British War Cabinet, brought to the notice of the First Sea Lord and others the importance of stopping the transportation of Swedish iron ore from

[1] *Official History. Naval Operations*, Vol. V, p. 340.

Narvik to Germany, *adding that it was necessary to prepare it.*[1]
That was the beginning of British planning. It is not even
mentioned in the Judgement.

No mention either is made in the Judgement of Mr. Churchill's
very important Memorandum to the Cabinet of September
29, 1939, in which he explains how vitally important to Germany is the supply of the Swedish ore, and how its interception
or interruption during the winter months, *i.e.*, from October
to April, would greatly reduce her power of resistance. Nor
is a hint given in the Judgement of Mr. Churchill's warning
to the Cabinet in the same Memorandum that, if the supplies
of ore from Narvik to Germany—which had temporarily abated
through Swedish action—started again *more drastic action would
be needed.* The First Lord's Instruction of the same date to the
Assistant Chief of the Naval Staff to consider and report on the
point on the Norwegian coast at which traffic should be stopped,
is also entirely ignored in the Judgement.[2]

The importance of the Memoranda and Minutes lies in
the fact that the British Government began to plan their
major offensive in Norway a fortnight before the Germans.
Mr. Churchill was already warning the Cabinet that, to make it
effective before the winter months, a breach of Norwegian
neutrality might become necessary. There was, of course,
nothing heinous in that from the point of view of the planners.
Their business was to carry out their instructions and to plan
and prepare, because at that stage no one could possibly fore-
see what the attitude of Norway would be, or whether some
German aggression might produce a legitimate excuse or justification for putting the British operation in force. The German
planners were in exactly the same position. They knew, as our
planners knew, that the execution of their plan *might* involve
an act of aggression. On the other hand, they knew from our
Official History how near Britain had been to a breach of Norwegian neutrality in the First World War ; such a breach, they
might argue, would provide a reasonable pretext for their plan.
That was the position, on both sides until mid-March. In
short, both sides were planning an operation, which might or
might not involve an act of aggression.

[1] Winston Churchill, *The Gathering Storm*, p. 421.
[2] *Ibid.*, pp. 422–24.

The omission to mention this part of the story in the Judgement is the more inexplicable because the whole story was told to the House of Commons by Mr. Churchill in April, 1940,[1] and it was a matter of public knowledge.

The whole burden then of the Tribunal's account of this stage of the Norwegian campaign is to show that the Germans were already planning an act of aggression for which punishment must be meted out. They do not mention any of the evidence that the Allies were doing the same thing at the same time, indeed did so even before the Germans ! Any soldier or sailor or airman could have told this International *Military* Tribunal that in fact both sides were merely exercising reasonable foresight and prescience, and that neither side was at that stage in any way culpable. But there is no evidence in the Judgement that naval, military or air advice was taken on such points. Mr. Churchill's memoranda, as the Government revealed when I pressed for information, were not submitted to the Nuremberg judges.

We see from these omissions how gravely the case of the vanquished was prejudiced compared with the victors.

The Stage of Preparation

By the end of the year 1939 the work of planning and preparation on both sides was far advanced ; but still we find the Tribunal piling up the case against the Germans, while forgetting to consider how far it was conditioned by the Allies. The Judgement records how in mid-December, 1939, Raeder, Rosenberg, and eventually Hitler himself saw Quisling, who put forward a plan for a *coup d'état* in Norway. This suggests that Hitler was seeking an excuse, such as a *coup d'état* might provide, for an entry into Norway by invitation. But he was cautious on this occasion and said he would still prefer a neutral attitude on the part of Norway.

But, the Judgement does not contain a word of Mr. Churchill's Memorandum to the War Cabinet dated December 16, which opens by stating that the effectual stopping of Norwegian ore supplies to Germany ranks as *a major offensive operation of war*. Any detached person would think this a supremely important

[1] Winston Churchill, *The Gathering Storm*, p. 421 and pp. 474–5 ; also *Hansard*, Commons, April 11, 1940.

piece of evidence for the Tribunal, for it places the British plan
on the same level of importance as the German plan, which is
so severely condemned as a crime in law in the Judgement.
Remembering the extract from Mahan's *History* (p. 70), it
becomes evident that the projected blow against Germany's
steel output was as important to the Sea Powers (Great Britain
and France) as the occupation of Norway was to the Land
Power (Germany). How important it was is shown in the remainder of this long and prescient Memorandum which may
be summarized in the following manner : Mr. Churchill described how this was the only measure open to us for months to
come which would give so good a chance of abridging the waste
and destruction of the war or even of preventing the slaughter
which would result from the grapple of the main armies. Most
interesting too, was his examination of the countermeasures
which Germany was likely to take if we were to stop the Narvik
supplies, including perhaps a German domination of the Scan-
dinavian peninsula, the spreading of the war to Norway and
Sweden, involving perhaps the despatch of British and French
troops to those countries. He concluded that we had more to
gain than Germany from a German attack on Scandinavia.

The most important point, however, from the point of view
of the German trials was Mr. Churchill's conclusion. He said
that ' the final tribunal is our own conscience ' and proceeded
to an impassioned appeal that we, who were fighting the battle
of the small countries, should not allow them to tie our hands in
the struggle for rights and freedom. The letter of the law must
not obstruct those responsible for its enforcement. Humanity,
and not legality, must be our guide. Thus far, Mr. Churchill.

The Cabinet refused to be moved by these arguments from
their policy of neutrality. All they were willing to accept
from the advice rendered by the tempestuous First Lord,
was the authorization of diplomatic protests to Norway about
misuse of her territorial waters. They also allowed the military
examination of the implications of possible commitments in
Scandinavia, the preparation of plans for landing a force at
Narvik for the sake of Finland—then fighting the Russian
invader—and consideration of the military consequences of a
German occupation of Southern Norway.

All this underlines the fact that the British plan, which had been begun in September, was by then recognized to be ' *a major offensive operation of war* '. Yet the Tribunal never even mentioned it in its published Judgement. It was truly a major operation, not only on account of the effect it was expected to have in reducing the German power of waging war, but also because of the repercussions it was likely to have throughout Scandinavia ; it led, almost at once, to the preparation of considerable allied forces for use there. These proceedings also show the pressure the War Cabinet were under from their most powerful colleague, the future Prime Minister and National Leader, to persuade them to a technical act of aggression liable to set all Scandinavia ablaze—a ' crime ', to use Nuremberg's extravagant language, for which the Germans were destined to be so severely condemned by the Tribunal. Not a single word of it appears in the Nuremberg Judgement.

Expansion of Allied Planning

The Judgement records how, on January 27, 1940, General Keitel produced a Memorandum on the plans for the invasion of Norway, which Hitler had placed under his direction. No reference is made, however, to the important developments in the plans of the Allies which took place on February 5, at Paris, where the Supreme War Council of the Allies, attended by Mr. Neville Chamberlain, Lord Halifax and Mr. Churchill himself, approved plans for the preparation of three or four allied divisions for service in Finland, and for persuading Norway and Sweden to permit the passage of supplies and reinforcements to the Finns and ' *incidentally to get hold of the Gällivare ore-field* '.[1] From then on the preparations for despatch of allied troops to Norway were intensified.

Up to this point there had been no major violation of Norwegian neutrality by either side, beyond the sinking of a few merchant ships in Norwegian waters, which are mentioned by Mr. Churchill but without details. At any rate, there had been no serious protest by the Norwegian Government against breach of neutrality.

The Approach of the Crisis

On February 16, 1940, however, there occurred an incident, which again is not even mentioned in the Nuremberg

[1] Winston Churchill, *The Gathering Storm*, pp. 442–43.

Judgement, although, as Mr. Churchill records, it ' sharpened everything in Scandinavia ', namely the rescue by a cutting-out party from H.M.S. *Cossack* from the German ship *Altmark* in Norwegian territorial waters of a number of British seamen who had been rescued from torpedoed merchant ships. The impor-tance of this gallant exploit was that it came at a moment when the German preparations for invading Norway were well advanced and Hitler was seeking a pretext which would ' justify ' his launching it. It spurred him to action. Four days later, on February 20, on Keitel's suggestion, the Führer (as recorded by Mr. Churchill but not by the Tribunal) sent for General von Falkenhorst and gave him command of the Norwegian expedition. From his verbal appreciation of the situation, as described by the General at the Nuremberg trials, it looks as though Hitler had got wind of the allied plans formu-lated at Paris ; Hitler said he was informed that the Allies in-tended to land in Scandinavia and explained in some detail how this would interfere in his own plans in Western Europe by threatening the German weak flank in the Baltic.[1]

The ' spur to action ' given by the *Altmark* episode would seem also to have inspired Hitler's directive of March 1, 1940, which is mentioned on page 28 of the Judgement. He there puts as his objects that ' this operation should prevent British encroachment on Scandinavia and the Baltic ; further it should guarantee our ore base in Sweden, and give our Navy and Air Force a wider start against Britain '. It will be noticed that the first two reasons were purely defensive ones and only the third was offensive though even that could be described as an ' offensive-defensive ' operation. Although the Tribunal men-tioned the directive, it apparently had no effect on its refusal to admit that the German invasion had any defensive element at all. But then the Tribunal had no military advisers so far as I am aware.

However, the *Altmark* episode against which the Norwegians (unnoticed by the Nuremberg Tribunal) protested vehemently does not seem to have given Hitler the pretext he was seeking for launching the invasion of Norway, for he continued to hesi-tate until the middle of March as to what pretext he would

[1] *Ibid.*, p. 446.

adopt. Perhaps the effective British reply to the Norwegian protest convinced him.

The Crisis

By the beginning of April, 1940, the preparations for the major offensive operation in Norway had been completed by both camps. Neither side had given the other an easy excuse for launching their expedition, and by a coincidence the two operations were launched almost simultaneously without any pretext having been found. Although the German fleet made the first move by a diversion in the North Sea on April 7 to cover the movements of transports, the actual landing, that is to say the German major offensive operation, did not take place until *April 9, Twenty-four hours before that, namely between 4.30 and 5 a.m. on April 8*, the British minefields had been laid in the West Fjord near Narvik !

Remarks

The story of the Norwegian Campaign, as told in the Nuremberg Judgement, contains few if any inaccuracies. It is the truth and nothing but the truth—but it is not the whole truth. It is indeed only half the story ; and by omitting the other half it is distorted, not history. By adding the part of the story that has been omitted at the Trial it has been shown that, from the start of planning to the German invasion, both Great Britain and Germany were keeping more or less level in their plans and preparations. Britain actually started planning a little earlier, partly owing to Mr. Churchill's prescience, and partly perhaps because she had a better and more experienced system of Higher Control of the War than Germany. Throughout the period of preparations the planning continued normally. Both plans could be classed as major offensive operations of war. Neither plan could be initiated without either an invitation from Norway, who naturally preferred to preserve her neutrality as in the First World War, or alternatively incurring the odium of perpetrating an aggression. This bore heavily on the British because they had stood by smaller nations against aggression ; the essence of their plan was to stop the German supplies of Gällivare ore during the winter before the Baltic unfroze, and in the matter of aggression Great Britain had a reputation to lose owing to her correctness and restraint in *e.g.* the First World War. Hitler, however, who must have guessed the pressure to which the British Government was exposed to make them take a risk, held back as long as he dared.

Who took the decision for action and in what circumstances, does not seem to have been published in either country. But both plans were executed almost simultaneously, Britain being twenty-four hours ahead in this so-called act of aggression, if the term is really applicable to either side. At any rate, if it was applicable to one belligerent, it was equally applicable to the other, and that is where the Nuremberg Tribunal, by describing only the German side of the campaign, went so grievously astray.

Imagine that the situation had been reversed, that Germany had won the war and had set up such a Tribunal, with the same Charter, to try its enemies : does anyone doubt the result, so far as the Norwegian campaign is concerned ? All that Mr. Churchill said about the deadly effect on Germany of a success-ful mining of the Norwegian Leads, about its being a major offensive operation of war, about the early start in planning and about our twenty-four hour lead in execution would have been trotted out. The operation would have been declared an act of aggression and everyone concerned in it—members of the War Cabinet, Chiefs of Staff, Joint Planning Committees, Admirals, Generals and Air Marshals galore would, on the Nuremberg analogy, have been tried, condemned and executed! How should we and posterity have felt about it ? Politics and legal Trials of this sort do not mix. They are grievous errors for which we all pay dearly in years of waiting—waiting for a Peace which cannot be born of vengeance but must flow from justice.

CHAPTER FIVE

THE JAPANESE TRIALS

IN debating the Tokyo trials on May 19 the House of Lords was breaking new ground. For two or three years, only scraps of information had been received from rare press messages and from travellers' tales, though in mid-November, 1948, a summary of the sentences had been published. This caused uneasiness. It was only in the last half of April, 1949, however, that, through the good offices of Major-General Piggott, I received a mass of papers bearing on the Trials in general and more particularly on the case of Mr. Shigemitsu, the Ambassador of Japan in London before the war.

In company with Major-General Piggott and other British and American friends, I had tried to help Mr. Shigemitsu in 1946 when we first heard of his plight, and again in 1948 when we received news of his conviction.

Perusal of the new papers, which had come from Mr. George A. Furness, Shigemitsu's American Counsel, showed that there was at least a prima facie case for reconsideration of the sentence on Shigemitsu, and perhaps on others. Shocked by the sentence of seven years' imprisonment on Shigemitsu, I reluctantly decided to add to my work by taking the matter up, and put down a motion for Debate in the Lords. Three weeks before this Debate I learned that a huge mass of material had arrived in the Foreign Office, and Lord Henderson, Parliamentary Under-Secretary of State, very kindly gave me access to it. The papers made a pile of double-spaced foolscap 30 feet high, and included a Majority Judgement of 1,600 pages, Minority Judgements totalling over 1,500 pages, and 48,000 pages of evidence. For the next three weeks every hour that I could spare was spent in the Foreign Office Library, where I received all possible help. Naturally, I could not (nor need I for this purpose) read all this material. But few, if any, in Britain have scanned as much of it as I did. Even so, I had hardly touched the historical part of the judgement, which may be of importance, when I spoke in the Debate on May 19. It is worth mentioning that the Government have since promised to place copies of the majority and minority Judgements in the Library of the House of Lords, as suggested by me as an interim measure, and to consider later whether there is a case for having it printed. This is a good example of the danger that the functions of parliamentary Government can be obstructed as easily by excess of information as by its lack.

Since Mr. Shigemitsu, to whose sterling character a number of well-known British and American citizens have paid spontaneous tribute, was still in durance vile, there was no time to lose. In rising on May 19 in the House of Lords, therefore, to call attention to the present situation in Japan in relation to war crimes trials I gave special attention to his case.

I said : " To-day, under inescapable impulse of personal conscience and public duty, I call attention to the Tokyo trials of war criminals generally, and, in that framework, to the plight of one of their victims, an old and true friend of this country, Mamoru Shigemitsu, who was Japanese Ambassador here before the war. If I had time I would expand on his love of peace, his patriotism, his vision to see that Japan's higher interests lay in peace and friendship especially with this country and America, his courage to press his views on his Government, even when they were unpopular, and the aura of integrity and goodness that surrounded the man. But, more eloquent than anything I can say, are the first and last lines of the dissenting judgement of the learned Netherlands Justice at the Tokyo trials, Mr. Roling. His first words were : ' The evidence laid before this Tribunal reveals Shigemitsu as a diplomatist and statesman who worked for peace rather than for war . . .' The learned Justice's last words in his judgement were : ' Summarizing, the accused Mamoru Shigemitsu should be acquitted on all charges brought against him.' "

My tribute to Shigemitsu's personality and especially to his ' aura of integrity and goodness, somewhat inexplicably aroused the indignation of the Lord Chancellor in his speech at the end of the Debate. He was staggered that I could use such a phrase, and in justification he proceeded to quote what he described as just ' one telegram ', dated August 5, 1940. It was, he said, sent by Shigemitsu, who was then Japanese Ambassador in London to his Foreign Secretary in Japan, Matsuoka, and read as follows :

" . . . in order to establish our position in Greater East Asia it would be necessary to consider measures for gaining the maximum benefits at the minimum loss by carrying them out at the direct expense of small nations (for instance, France and Portugal, although indirectly it may turn out to be at the expense of Britain and America) and by avoiding conflict with other countries so as not to make many enemies at once but to dispose of them one by one." Commenting on this quotation, the Lord Chancellor made the following observation : " That man, you see, advocated hitting first at the ' little ones '. He included France in that description. France being then occupied and unable to defend herself. This is the man whom we are asked to think of as possessing this ' aura of integrity '."

These remarks received a wide publicity—more than they deserved—and were probably broadcast all over the world. Without an opportunity to check the facts they could not have been answered on the spot even if time had been available. But as the unfortunate Shigemitsu is still in prison, they must be answered here. First, it should be noted that this ' one telegram ' was not a telegram, but an extract occupying 8 or 9 lines of a long telegram of nearly 100 lines. Worse, the extract had been wrenched from its context. Before reading the ' telegram ' the Lord Chancellor had admitted that Shigemitsu was found *Not Guilty* in respect of his work as an Ambassador, and that an Ambassador must have great latitude ; but he omitted to mention that the extract had been brought to the notice of the Tokyo Tribunal by the Prosecution as possible evidence against Shigemitsu on Count I, Participation in Conspiracy to Wage War. He also omitted to mention that the Tribunal had examined it, not in isolation, but in the proper context of the telegram of August 5, as a whole. And the Tribunal had done so in the setting of a summary, several pages in length, of Shigemitsu's many telegrams in which he advised successive Japanese Governments during the two years before Japan entered the war. Neither did Lord Jowitt state that the Judgement, where it deals with this matter, contains nothing to support his interpretation of the extract. Instead it paves the way to the finding that Shigemitsu was *not* one of the conspirators, *that he repeatedly gave advice to the Japanese Foreign Office which was opposed to the policies of the conspirators, and that*

he was not guilty on Count I.[1] The fact that the dissenting learned
Justices of France and the Netherlands—two of the ' little
ones '—both found Shigemitsu not guilty on all charges is an
interesting commentary on the Lord Chancellor's interpretation.

Viscount Jowitt was of course under no obligation to mention
these considerations since his only object was to counter and
discredit my tribute to Shigemitsu's moral integrity—and the
Tribunal had been set up to investigate crime and not morals.
But the line between the two is not sharp ; and if Shigemitsu
was to blame over this telegram, it could hardly have escaped
comment in one or other of the Judgements.

My own tribute to Shigemitsu's integrity was based, not
on my interpretation of a short extract from just ' one
telegram ' divorced from its context, but on long and repeated
conversations with him, sometimes in company with others,
including the late Lord Lloyd, then Secretary of State for the
Colonies (whose estimate of Shigemitsu was as high as my own),
and sometimes alone. Moreover, my opinion is strikingly confirmed by statements, which, as mentioned later, were sent to
the Tribunal independently by no less than sixteen eminent
British and American citizens. These between them cover the
whole of his career as an Ambassador. They contain phrases
just as cordial as the one to which the Lord Chancellor took
exception, *e.g.*, ' *a man of personal integrity and idealism*, a view
that was shared by most members of the American Embassy
at Moscow' (Loy Henderson, United States Diplomat) ; ' *definitely a liberal, progressive and altruistic humanitarian* in his approach
to international relations ' (Joseph Davies, United States Ambassador) ; ' a man most friendly to peace between our countries ' (Mr. Winston Churchill) ; ' Mr. Shigemitsu has won
personal respect everywhere in London ' (*Times* Leading
Article, June 20, 1941) ; ' Mr. Shigemitsu was generally regarded as a man of high character ' (Mr. R. A. Butler, Parlia-
mentary-Under-Secretary of State, Foreign Office, 1940) ; ' I
can recall no instance during my fifteen years in the Embassy
at Tokyo, that any commentary was made by the Embassy to
the Department of State on Mr. Shigemitsu that was not com-
plimentary and favourable to him ' (Eugene H. Dooman,

---

[1] Author's italics.

United States Diplomat) ; ' He was essentially a man of peace
and one quite incapable, in my judgement, of any action, open
or underhand, that would lead to war ' (Lord Sempill). To
these can be added the appreciation of some of the speakers in
the Debate including the Earl of Perth who described him as
' a loyal and patriotic man ' and heartily supported my plea
for revision of the sentence.

All these men knew Shigemitsu well ; and it is impossible
that, without some such qualities as ascribed to him, so remarkable a collection of tributes from the countries of his former
enemies could have been written. On the issue of Shigemitsu's
moral qualities, therefore, his reputation has nothing to fear
from the remarks of the only speaker in the House of Lords
Debate to say a word against him. Having established this, I
turned to the less exciting question of my request for Papers—no
mere formality in this instance.

The Publication of Papers

" Although more than six months have passed ", I said,
" since the publication of the Judgement and findings of the
Tokyo Tribunal, the Government have published nothing at
all so far as I am aware. I must thank Lord Henderson for
allowing me access to the one typescript of the judgement and
findings in the Foreign Office Library. It is many times longer
than the Nuremberg White Paper. It is not an easy method,
having to get one's information in that way, and check it. The
Majority Judgement covers more than a thousand pages of
close typescript and the three dissenting Judgements are, in
the aggregate, longer still, but they are of considerable importance. I realize that, in present conditions, it will take some
time to produce a White Paper similar to the Nuremberg Report, though it must be done in the case of so important and
historic a document, and I must ask particularly for an answer
on that point. I suggest that pending the print, a type-written
copy of the Judgements, including the dissenting Judgements,
should be placed in the Library. I have given notice of that."

The Lord Chancellor undertook to arrange for the Majority
and Minority Judgements to be placed in the House of Lords

Library, and promised to consult at a later stage with the
Foreign Secretary as to whether there was a case for printing
them.

" In this country ", I continued, " what little information
has been published about the trials, is not edifying. In America
more has been published and it is less edifying. Private communications and impressions from Tokyo are the least edifying
of all. As a leading article in the *Washington Post* of January
11, 1949, put it : ' It is more and more evident to us that the
good name of justice, let alone of the United States, has been
compromised by the War criminal cases in Tokyo.'

" The Proclamation establishing the Tribunal was issued on
January 19, 1946, and the trials have taken about two and a
half years. That is very hard on the accused and indeed on
everyone. But it is not surprising. There were eleven judges,
and twenty-five accused who were all pronounced guilty.
Seven, including six generals, were sentenced to death by
hanging ; sixteen were imprisoned for life ; one was sentenced
to twenty years' imprisonment and one, namely Shigemitsu,
to seven years' imprisonment. There were, as I have already
mentioned, three dissenting judgements. They were delivered
by the learned French, Netherlands, and Indian justices respectively, which shows how controversial these trials must
have been. It all sounds very unwieldy and cumbersome and
not exactly the milieu in which men ought to be tried for their
lives.

" According to a notable dispatch in *The Times* of November
12, the President, Sir William Webb, the learned Australian
Justice, expressing an opinion differing in certain ways from
the majority judgement, said that the crimes of the persons
accused were far less heinous, varied and extensive than those
of the Germans accused at Nuremberg. He also expressed the
opinion that it might prove revolting to hang or shoot such
old men as are several of the accused. After some adverse remarks on the responsibility of the Emperor, who had been
granted immunity from trial, he went on to say : ' If in such
a case the court must by law impose capital punishment, the
prerogative of mercy would probably be exercised in order to
save the lives of the condemned '. In spite of that strong hint,
all the death sentences were carried out.

" According to *The Times* report, counsel for the defence protested vigorously against the Tribunal's refusal to read in open court the three dissenting opinions, and accused the court of unfairness in refusing to allow the defendants ' to know what is said touching their lives and liberties '. This is rather serious, because the dissenting Judgements, individually and collectively are very critical of the Majority Judgement. Much more has appeared in reputable British and American newspapers. I have quoted only *The Times* and the *Washington Post* . . . ; it is sufficient to mention the titles of leading articles, such as ' Injustice in Tokyo ' and ' Shigemitsu Travesty ' These reports, which have not been challenged, were sufficiently serious to stir me to very close scrutiny of the judgements, as close a scrutiny as I could manage of this enormous mass of documents for which I had to go to the Foreign Office Library. That scrutiny did not reassure me.

" There is one feature in the Tokyo trials which distinguishes it markedly from Nuremberg. At the latter nearly all the defendants convicted of serious crimes against peace were also found guilty of serious crimes against humanity, for which they would have received death sentences anyway, as the greater crime included the less. That was true also of the seven men sentenced to death at Tokyo : they were all condemned for crimes against humanity as well as crimes against peace. But in the case of the sixteen life imprisonment sentences, no fewer than fourteen of the accused were sentenced only for political crimes—I mean by that, crimes against peace. In addition, Togo was sentenced to twenty years' imprisonment, making fifteen of these cases altogether. In the case of the Tokyo trials the historical background of the trials, which I raised a fortnight ago in discussing the Nuremberg trials (and dealt with in the previous chapter of this book), may become important, but until we have easier access to documents not much can be said on that point, which I reserve.

" The matter has to be considered, however, and all the more carefully because the procedure in findings of fact at the time of the trial was severely criticized by the learned French judge, and this was one of the many reasons for his dissent. After stating that the guarantees, which the law of nations grant the defendants, include ' oral deliberations outside of all influence

bearing on all produced evidence among all the judges who sat
at the trials,' he continued ; ' All the part of the Judgement
relative to the findings of fact were proposed by a drafting
committee and submitted by the latter as its preparations
progressed, first to a committee of seven judges called the
' Majority '.   Copy of this draft was also distributed to the four
other members of the Tribunal.   The latter were called upon to
submit their own views to the majority in view of their discussion, and should the case arise, for modification of the draft.
*But the eleven judges were never called to meet to discuss orally a part
of or in its entirety this part of the judgements.*[1]

"   I am referring to the factual part :   ' Only the part of the
draft relative to individual cases was the object of oral discussion '.   To the layman who knows nothing of these methods
of procedure, it would be rather interesting to know whether
this system of majority and minority groups is usual.   I imagine
that one has to adopt all sorts of expedients when there is such
a large court."

No reply was made during the Debate on any of these points,
which is the more striking because the Government had a
diplomatic mission in Tokyo throughout the trials, and must
have received reports.

Conspiracy

"   On one point the Tokyo Tribunal seems to have imitated
the Nuremberg trial rather too closely—namely, in trying to
establish that there was a conspiracy in Japan to do all these
wicked things.   As I read the Majority Judgement I felt that the
arguments on this point were rather thin, and the dissenting
Judgements strongly confirm that view. . . .   I will read two
short extracts.   Here is one from the French dissenting judgement :   ' No direct proof was furnished concerning the forma-
tion among individuals known, on a known date, at a specified
point, of a plot, the object of which was to assure Japan the
domination, unaccepted by its inhabitants, of some part of the
world.   The only thing proved is the existence among certain
influential classes of the Japanese nation of the desire to seat

----

[1] Author's italics.

at all costs the domination of Japan upon other parts of East Asia.'

" The second extract is from the judgement of the Honourable Justice Pal, the learned Indian Justice, who said : ' The case of the accused before us cannot in any way be likened to the case either of Napoleon or Hitler. The constitution of Japan was fully working. The sovereign, the Army, and the Civil officials all remained connected as usual and in normal ways with the society. The constitution of the State remained fashioned as before in relation to the will of the society. . . . These accused came into power constitutionally and only to work the machinery provided by the constitution. . . . These persons did not usurp any power.' And so on.

" This makes it look as though the Japanese, though stupid and sometimes wicked, did not conspire. During my own association with the Japanese in the years between the wars there was no change at any time in the personnel one met at international conferences. The various representatives were always very much the same. The point is of importance, because the accused with the exception of only three, including Shigemitsu, were convicted on Count I, of conspiracy, which was treated as the worst of the political crimes. ' Conspiracy ' appears in a very large number of the individual findings. With conspiracy in Count I went wars of aggression, and some of the dissenting Judgements point out how desperately controversial the question of defining ' aggression ' has been in the past. I have myself seen three great efforts of the League of Nations fail largely on the question of aggression, and I have never yet seen a definition that could pass muster, at any rate, of the Service staffs. . . .

" All these points seem to me to tend towards the desirability of a revision of the sentences. Although the case against Shigemitsu is the only one I pretend to have examined carefully, I am told that there are grave doubts about some of the others. For instance, the sentence of death on Hirota is very much criticized, particularly in Japan, where the people cannot understand why he was condemned to death."

That part of the speech aroused little criticism during the Debate, except that the Lord Chancellor resented some of it as an implied attack on Lord Patrick, the British Judge, who was one of the majority and to whom he paid a well-deserved tribute in which I joined. Of course, it had never entered into my mind to attack individual judges at Tokyo any more than at Nuremberg, especially Lord Patrick, who I knew had been ill during much of the trial. As in the case of my speech on the German trials a fortnight earlier my charge was directed against the policy of these international War Crimes Trials and those who conceived them, on the ground that they could not attain that optimum standard of justice which is essential for the trial of men's lives and a nation's reputation before history.

Most of the weaknesses of the Nuremberg trials were repeated and exaggerated at Tokyo. Instead of four judges there were eleven. Instead of one short dissenting Judgement, there were three long ones—to say nothing of the President's pronouncement mentioned on page 85. So sharp was the rift that, as mentioned, the Tribunal was divided into a Majority and a Minority, and so wide were the differences of opinion that the members of the Minority felt it necessary to express their views in immensely long and closely argued dissenting Judgements. And, as we shall see in Chapter VII, the American counsel for the defence were so strongly moved that they combined to send to General MacArthur a formidable criticism of the fairness of the trials. Again, it was a trial by the victors of the vanquished. While the accused Tojo was awaiting his sentence of death he was asked by a reporter what he thought about the trials, and his reply was ' I can only say it was a victor's trial ' (*Nippon Times*, November 13, 1948). That was no more than the truth. Once more, also, there was the disconcerting fact that one of the Judges represented a country that could be accused of many of the crimes listed in the indictment.

Anyone who can conceive that the judgements, however fair they may be in fact, will go down in history as an expression of justice and will be accepted in Japan as such must be something more than blind. For already in Japan, and even in Europe and America, there are widespread doubts about several of the verdicts and sentences, apart from the case of Shigemitsu. His case I shall examine, just as I examined the Norwegian Campaign with regard to Nuremberg, as a sample of what is defended as a fair trial by official sponsors of this system.

CHAPTER SIX

SHIGEMITSU

I NOW come to Shigemitsu and I quote from my speech which remained largely unreported in the press on May 19, 1949. Again, in my comments, I have added new material, no less perturbing. " Much of the criticism of these trials, private as well as public, centres around the case of Shigemitsu, where there seems to me to be a strong prima facie case for revision. American papers and broadcasts have stated repeatedly that the Chief Prosecutor, Mr. Joseph B. Keenan, has declared that Shigemitsu should not have been put on trial, let alone convicted, and that he disagrees with the International Court in imposing a seven-year term of imprisonment. He also says that, but for the Russians, Shigemitsu would neither have been tried nor convicted.[1] From the sponsor of the very tough indictment made at the beginning of the trial, that is a strong statement. It does not surprise me, because I heard rumours of the same kind as early as 1946, which have since been confirmed by American counsel for the defence.

" His Excellency Mamoru Shigemitsu, to give him his full title, was, as I have said, Japanese Ambassador in London from 1938 until the outbreak of war with Japan on December 7, 1941. He was a worthy successor to a distinguished line of Japanese Ambassadors, and was much respected here, even during the difficult months before the war, when he was doing his best to avert that catastrophe. I have in my hands more than a dozen tributes, prepared as evidence by well-known people, and sent under affidavit to Tokyo, to his work for peace, here and elsewhere. They include an extract from a speech in secret session

---

[1] Russia only became entitled to a seat on the Tokyo Tribunal by declaring war on Japan a few days before the war came to an end and in breach of her non-aggression pact. Mr. Byrnes tells a strange story of a formula which he and his staff had to concoct to try and justify the aggression. Although Japan surrendered a few days after the declaration of war the Russian forces entered Manchuria and proceeded to loot the country. James F. Byrnes, *Speaking Frankly*, Chapter II.

by Mr. Winston Churchill, and statements by Mr. R. A. Butler, and three British Ambassadors, Lord Killearn, Sir Robert Craigie, and Sir Francis Lindley. The latter asks me to say that he considers the sentence of Shigemitsu the grossest miscarriage of justice. The list of those who have paid tribute includes six American diplomats, among them Mr. Joseph E. Davies, Mr. Kennedy, and Mr. Joseph Grew. Lord Killearn was anxious to make a short statement to-day. I understand that he has authorized Lord Sempill to communicate the gist of what he intended to say. Lord Altrincham regrets very much that at the last moment he has been prevented from coming here to put in a word for Shigemitsu.

" My own statement was concerned solely with the first half of the war when, in conjunction with the late Lord Lloyd and one or two others, with the permission, of course, of the Foreign Secretary, I was in close touch with Shigemitsu on how to avert the extension of the war to Japan.

Conspiring Wars of Aggression

" There is no need to develop that theme, because—I hope with some aid from the documents sent to Japan—Shigemitsu was pronounced not guilty on the charge of conspiring or instigating wars of aggression ; that is to say, he was not found guilty on the most serious charge, which would certainly have involved his death. To quote the majority findings : ' He was not one of the conspirators. Indeed, he repeatedly gave advice to the Foreign Office which was opposed to the policies of the conspirators.'

Waging Aggressive War

" But Shigemitsu was found guilty of waging aggressive war, on which the majority finding records : ' He waged no war of aggression until he became Foreign Minister in April, 1943, by which time his country was deeply involved in a war which would greatly affect its future.' To the layman, that charge of waging war after 1943, is answered very effectively in the long dissenting judgement of the learned Mr. Justice Roling, whom I have already quoted. In April, 1943, when Shigemitsu joined the Cabinet, he could not have been waging war of aggression, for the simple reason that the aggression had run out. It had been planned before the war, and had failed. Japan—and, indeed, the whole Axis—was by then fighting a defensive war. The battle of Midway Island had been lost ; Japan had been thrown back in New Guinea and in the Solomon Islands ; the Allies had landed in North Africa, and the Germans were retreating in Russia.

" Moreover, Shigemitsu had entered the Cabinet as Foreign Minister, with the object of promoting peace, on which Mr. Justice Roling cites a good deal of evidence—for instance, approaches to the Swedish Minister, an attempt to secure Russian mediation, talks from the very early days of his tenure of office, continued until his retirement, with Kido the Emperor's adviser, and reports on peace prospects to the Emperor himself. All that I get from Mr. Justice Roling's judgement, but I could not see anything about it in the Majority findings . . . I do not think they are there.

" Mr. Justice Roling says : ' He who assumes public office in order to oppose that war, who accepts his appointment in order to promote peace, cannot and should not be accused of waging an aggressive war.' Mr. Justice Roling scouts as untenable the contention of the Majority Judgement that the mere fact of entering a Cabinet as Foreign Minister, as Shigemitsu did in 1943, is *per se* a crime. And I think he is right. The majority findings say of Shigemitsu that on taking office ' he played a principal part in waging that war until he resigned on April 13, 1945.' You can search the majority findings, and you cannot find what that ' principal part ' is, either in the general Judgement relating to all defendants, or in the verdict relating to Shigemitsu.

" As one who has lived with Cabinets in two major wars, in the first as a Secretary and in the second as a Minister of Cabinet rank, I am a little puzzled to know what ' principal part ' he can have played outside his own sphere. For example, I have never considered myself responsible for events like the loss of the *Prince of Wales* and *Repulse* of which I knew nothing beforehand. The point was raised in the Dardanelles Commission in the First World War, when Mr. McKenna and some others repudiated all responsibility for the naval attack on the Dardanelles. On that the Dardanelles Commission's pro-

nouncement was as follows : ' We consider that the responsibility of those members of the Cabinet who did not attend the
meetings of the War Council was limited to the fact that they
had delegated their responsibility to their colleagues who
attended those meetings.'

" Of course, that limitation on the responsibility of civilian
Ministers applies especially in Japan where the military authorities were so dominant. As Mr. Comyns Carr, just back from
Tokyo, told the Royal Empire Society the other day : ' The
War and Navy Ministers in the Japanese Government were
not selected by the Prime Minister : they were appointed by
the three senior officers in each of the two Services.' These
officers, by the simple process of refusing to appoint a Minister,
could prevent any Government of which they did not approve
from ever being formed. They could smash it by withdrawing
their Minister and refusing to appoint another. That shows
very graphically the position of the military authorities.

" Moreover, I submit that the precedents are against the
Majority Judgement. Your Lordships will remember the
Nuremberg findings in the case of Speer, who was Minister of
Munitions. This is the extract : ' His activities in charge of
German armament production were in aid of the war effort
in the same way that other productive enterprises did in the
waging of war ; but the Tribunal is not prepared to find that
such activities involve engaging in the common plan to wage
aggressive war as charged under Count I or as waging aggressive
war as charged under Count II.'

" While we are on precedents, what a precedent Tokyo has
created ! Any statesman in any country joining a War Cabinet
as Foreign Minister to get peace when his country is in trouble
will, in future, by the simple fact of doing so, be liable to condemnation by his enemies—nobody else will condemn him—of
waging aggressive war ! I submit that the majority findings on
Shigemitsu on the charge of waging aggressive war are so controversial as to support my demand for revision. In such
revision I think the minority findings should receive close
attention, and that Shigemitsu should receive the benefit of
the doubt."

The Lord Chancellor did not accept the view that by the time
Shigemitsu joined the Japanese Cabinet, the war had ceased

to be a war of aggression. It had begun as a war of aggression at Pearl Harbour and in his view a war of aggression it remained —presumably up to the last day when, reduced by the Atomic Bomb to the last gasp, Japan surrendered. The fact that Japan found she had ' bitten off more than she could chew ' made no difference. He did not say in so many words that he supported the contention of the Majority Judgement that by joining the Cabinet Shigemitsu was *ipso facto* waging a war of aggression, but he gave that impression.

As that is a legal question it had better be answered by a lawyer. Mr. Justice Roling deals with it in a long passage in his Dissenting Judgement : ' Although admitting that there may be grounds for mitigation of punishment in the case of a person entering a War Cabinet in order to end the war as soon as possible, it is contended in the Majority Judgement that the mere fact of entering such a Cabinet in the capacity of Foreign Minister, as Shigemitsu did in 1943, is *per se* a crime. It seems that this view is incorrect and untenable. *It would compel statesmen, who desire to work for peace, to abstain from holding positions in which they could achieve their desire. It would, in any war prevent anybody from joining his government unless he supported the war wholeheartedly.*[1] To enter a Cabinet, and to assume an office through which one obtains the power necessary to be able to work for peace, is a duty rather than a crime. . . .'

But the Lord Chancellor expressed doubts as to whether in fact Shigemitsu did join the Cabinet to try and make peace. He pointed out that Shigemitsu never said so himself. That is true, for the accused never said one word in Court! He did not elect to give evidence in his own defence. Here is what Mr. Roling says on that point : ' The accused Shigemitsu chose not to take the stand as a witness. Consequently, the Tribunal does not have in evidence his motives for entering the Cabinet as it does in the case of the accused Togo. It would however, be incorrect to conclude from this refusal to appear as a witness that, for fear of prejudicing himself, the individual in question did not see his way to explaining his actions. *This refusal may have been based on various grounds as, e.g., reluctance to be forced into a position where he might not be able to avoid compromising his co-*

___
[1] Author's italics.

defendants.[1] Consequently, no conclusion whatsoever should be drawn from a refusal by the accused to appear as a witness.'

The words in italics will appeal strongly to those who know Shigemitsu's loyal character. It is even more likely that he may have been apprehensive lest anything should be drawn out of him detrimental to his Emperor, who had called him to serve his country.

Later Mr. Roling develops a strong presumptive case to show that in all probability Shigemitsu did in fact join the Cabinet to work for peace. He shows, first, that up to that time he had been a strong opponent of wars of aggression and that in fact he did work for peace : ' From the evidence laid before the Tribunal concerning the attitude and the activities of the accused Shigemitsu before 1943, it clearly follows that he was opposed to a war of aggression and that he endeavoured to prevent such a war. . . . The evidence concerning Shigemitsu's activities as Foreign Minister in the Tojo and Koiso Cabinets shows that he did his best to end the existing war as early as possible. He approached the Swedish Minister, Bagge, for that purpose. (T. 34561). He sought promotion of peace through Russian mediation (T. 34551). He discussed the possibilities of peace with Kido (The Emperor's political adviser) ever since the early days of his tenure of office (T. 31069), and reported on his efforts in this direction to the Emperor (T. 31107).'

It is worth noting at this point that in his Petition to General MacArthur for revision of Shigemitsu's sentence, Mr. Furness, Shigemitsu's Counsel, expanded the evidence about his client's discussions with Kido : ' While still Ambassador to the Government of Nanking, he discussed peace with the Emperor's adviser Kido on April 11, 1942. (Dissent of Roling, J., p. 225). Kido testified from the time of his appointment until the day of the surrender, he worked with Shigemitsu until the termination of the war. (Exh. 3340, Tr. 31069). The first Conference recorded in his diary was on May 13, 1943, within a month of Shigemitsu's appointment (Exh. 3340, Tr. 31069). Again in January, 1944, Shigemitsu stated to Kido that he believed that unconditional surrender was unavoidable (Exh. 3340, Tr. 31073, also Tr. 31244). Kido's diary shows that they conferred again

[1] Author's italics.

on June 28, 1944, and he testified that they worked out a plan
under which Kido would assume responsibility for the Imperial
Court and Shigemitsu for the Government (Exh. 3340, Tr.
31075). They conferred on July 6 and 15 (Exh. 3340, Tr.
31106) and throughout the summer and fall of 1944. Another
Conference is recorded on March 8, 1945 (Exh. 3340,Tr. 31114).

The case is overwhelming. Shigemitsu did his utmost before
the war to prevent its outbreak, and during the war he did his
utmost to bring it to an end. The only point on which full
proof is lacking is that he joined the Cabinet for the specific
purpose of working for peace. On the other hand there is not
a scrap of evidence to show that he joined it for any other purpose. One must therefore ask oneself for what other reason he
could possibly have entered the Cabinet.

Shigemitsu cannot have joined the Japanese Government
for the express purpose of ' waging aggressive warfare '. He
was not a military man and was perfectly aware that he was
joining a militarist Cabinet which, as the Majority Judgement
records ' completely controlled Japan while he was Foreign
Minister ' ; he knew that on military questions he would not
be listened to. Besides, the war had gone wrong for Japan, as
he had always realized would happen.

During the four hours' conversation which I had with
him on March 22, 1941, as mentioned in my Statement to the
Tribunal, Shigemitsu said that although ' Japan would
give us a bad time at first, he was under no illusion as to the
ultimate danger to his country '. In April, 1943, when he was
asked to join the Cabinet we had had our ' bad time ' and the
ultimate danger to Japan was staring him in the face. It was not
a moment to attract an amateur strategist to embark on waging
aggressive war. But it *was* a moment for a far-sighted diplomat
and patriotic statesman to try and work for peace.

Another possible motive would be ambition. But the only
possible direction in which he could hope to achieve results was
in his own field of foreign policy. And in that field there was
no scope for obtaining powerful allies, as all the Great Powers
were already engaged in the war on one side or the other. The
only outlet for ambition, then, was in the direction of peace.
He could not have known in April, 1943. that even that outlet

was to become blocked before long by allied intransigence in the matter of unconditional surrender.

What motive, then, remained ? Loyalty, perhaps, to the Emperor who had called him to the task—as the Earl of Perth suggested during the Debate—and a spirit of ' my country right or wrong ! ' To those who like myself believe in the primitive virtues that would be a good motive ; but from the rulings of Nuremberg and Tokyo it seeems they are unfashionable. That motive however is consistent with Shigemitsu's patriotism and integrity (*pace* the Lord Chancellor !). Moreover, it is not inconsistent with a hope of working for peace by taking office.

By a process of elimination therefore, we arrive at a strong probability that Shigemitsu's motive in becoming Foreign Minister must have been to work for peace. As Mr. Justice Roling sums it up : ' There are numerous indications that Shigemitsu entered the War Cabinet with the purpose of achieving peace. If there is any doubt concerning his intentions, he should have the benefit of the doubt ', This, I always thought, is established law in the Anglo-Saxon countries.

On the rest of my remarks, e.g. on the difficulty, from my own experience, that Shigemitsu would have had in ' playing a principal part ' in waging aggressive warfare; on the responsibility of the non-military members of a Cabinet for military decisions as defined by the Dardanelles Commission in the First World War and generally accepted ; and on the precedent of Speer, the German Minister of Munitions, who was exonerated from a similar charge by the Nuremberg Tribunal, no criticism was made during the Debate.

Prisoners of War

" Now I come to the prisoner of war charges, which are the most serious," I said. " Shigemitsu was found not guilty on the more serious charge of authorizing or permitting or encouraging the committing of war crimes, or of crimes against humanity, but guilty on Count 55, that he ' deliberately and recklessly disregarded his legal duty to take steps to secure the observance and prevent breaches of the laws of war.

" Before coming to the details of this charge I must refer to a new principle (mentioned in Mr. Comyns Carr's talk to the Royal Empire Society) which did not arise at Nuremberg but which, as I understand him, was established for the first time at Tokyo. It seems that the Tribunal held that 'a Government and not merely its military commanders is responsible for the proper carrying out of the duties under the Hague and Geneva Conventions for the proper treatment of prisoners of war '— I have nothing to say on that— ' Even civilian members of the Government, if they are made aware that these Conventions are being broken in a wholesale manner by the forces for which they are responsible and take no proper steps to put matters right, are criminally responsible as well as the military leaders, to whose conduct it is directly due ' . . . I hope we shall be told under what power and by what authority this interpretation was adopted. Was it legal or was it not ? Neither the Fourth Hague Convention of 1907, nor the Regulations thereunder, nor the Geneva Convention of July 27, 1929, say more than that ' Prisoners of war are in the power of the hostile Government but not of the individuals or corps who capture them.'

" Every Government has to set up an inquiry office—which the Japanese did—but there is not a word as to what Minister or Department is to be responsible for administration and coordination. That is very properly left to each Government to decide for itself. As Mr. Justice Roling said : 'In every Government a division of labour is established, and where, as in Japan, special departments of the Government were charged with a special task, e.g., the War and Navy Ministries with the care for prisoners of war and civilian internees in occupied territory, the Home Ministry with the care for civilian internees in Japan proper, the Ministry of Overseas with the care for civilian internees in Formosa, Korea and Saghalin, the responsibility for not preventing violations of the rules of war should be limited to these officials especially indicated in the pertinent domestic law.'

" We shall see in a moment that the duties in regard to prisoners of war of Shigemitsu as Foreign Minister were very closely limited by Japanese law. He was practically no more than a Post Office. This interpretation hit him very hard. At any rate, neither Shigemitsu nor the other prisoners can possibly have known when they were in office that, after the war, their action or inaction would be interpreted by their enemies in that way. To invent a new interpretation during or just before the trial and to make it retrospective, does seem to be rather an extreme measure and rather a grim precedent for the future. There is an unsavoury flavour of vindictiveness about it."

Are civilian Ministers of a Government, who are made aware that Prisoners of War and kindred Conventions are being broken, criminally responsible? And are they so even if, like Shigemitsu, they have under the laws of their own country no power or right to interfere or even to make inquiries? I received no answer to these questions although I had given notice that I should raise the point. We were not told by what authority this new interpretation was given, nor whether it was new law, nor whether it is just or fair to try a man under an interpretation of a law that had not existed at the time when the alleged crime was committed.[1] M. Briand used to say that war was too serious a matter to be left to soldiers. It would seem that the law is too serious a matter to be left to lawyers. With this kind of precedent the politicians of all countries will have to be very careful lest they become the victims of some very curious new laws or some curiouser new interpretations of old laws, if they have the bad luck to be captured by their enemies or to lose a war!

Tojo's P.O.W. Responsibility

We must therefore turn to the very important points defining the overwhelming responsibilities in the matter of Prisoners of War and kindred questions which lay on Tojo. He was not only Shigemitsu's Chief as Prime Minister, but—holding also the office of Minister of War—exercised dictatorial powers in this matter. Shigemitsu's powers and functions in this class of question was limited to acting as a Post Office : to receive the protests of the Allies, to pass them on to the P.O.W. Department, and to retransmit the replies. There was practically no answer given to this part of my speech during the Debate :

" I shall now come to some very queer points about this verdict. I cannot help thinking that there must have been a slip somewhere. Here is the first. When Shigemitsu became Foreign Minister on April 17, 1943, he was a member of the

[1] For the bearing of the U.N. Declaration of Human Rights on this point see p. 131.

Government of Tojo, who had been War Minister from 1940 and, in addition, Prime Minister from October, 1941. He combined the two offices and retained them until July, 1944. If we turn to the majority findings on Tojo, we note that as Head of the War Ministry—to quote the text : '. . . he was charged with the care of prisoners of war and of civilian internees in the theatres of war. . . . Above all he was head of the Government which was charged with continuing responsibility for the care of prisoners and civilian internees'. The finding continues : ' The barbarous treatment of prisoners and internees was well known to Tojo. He took no adequate steps to punish offenders and to prevent the commission of war crimes in the future '. After two pages of detail of Tojo's criminal callousness and neglect, the finding states that Tojo was also responsible for preventing knowledge of the ill-treatment of prisoners reaching the outside world. He was found guilty under Count 54.

" From the general judgement on all the accused, we learn also that there was a bi-weekly conference of all bureau chiefs in the War Ministry—that was, on prisoners of war—which was presided over and usually attended by Tojo as War Minister, and by the Vice-Minister, at which the protests and the draft answers were brought up. Now if we turn to the findings on one Sato, Chief of the Military Affairs Bureau, and a member of the weekly Bureau conference, we find that ' Tojo presided at these meetings and he it was who decided that action or inaction should be taken in regard to the protests. Sato, his subordinate, could not initiate preventive action against the decision of his chief.' For that reason, I may add, Sato was found not guilty. Turning to Tojo, you can say he was completely and almost exclusively responsible for all decisions on prisoners of war questions. He was a soldier by profession, leader of what the majority judgement calls the conspirators who had brought Japan into the war, and a very tough man. He had been brought into office as Prime Minister in the manner I have described. He was not open to Western moral principles and concepts. His explanation of his attitude on the Bataan march was (to quote the majority finding) : ' that the commander of a Japanese Army in the field is given a mission in the performance of which he is not subject to specific orders from Tokyo.'

" Such then were the powers and responsibilities, and such was the character and temperament of the man under whom Shigemitsu, a civilian Foreign Minister, had to work for fifteen months in this prisoner of war business—that is to say, for just over half the time he was in office.   That, of course, was only a fraction of his duties.   They left very little responsibility or power to Shigemitsu, or to anybody else ; and they show how extraordinarily difficult it must have been for him to secure redress, however anxious he was for it.

" I suggest that the bearing of these difficulties on Shigemitsu's innocence are submerged in the Majority Judgement, for on reading the Judgement on Shigemitsu you find no mention of Tojo, and on reading the judgement of Tojo you find no mention of Shigemitsu.   There is not even a cross-reference or a hint to show how decisively his initiative must have been hampered by the fact that Tojo was his chief, as Prime Minister, who wielded these tremendous powers in prisoner of war questions, as War Minister, and was such a violent man.   It is all the worse because, broadly speaking, the findings are, in alphabetical order, so that the story of Tojo is not in the reader's mind when he reads the findings on Shigemitsu ; and the point has not been mentioned in the earlier general judgement.   That promotes a suspicion that it was not in the mind of the Tribunal either, or they could not have ignored it.   It looks as if one judge had written the findings on Tojo and another on Shigemitsu, and as if they had not been compared and ' stitched together ' properly.   I ask your Lordships to bear that in mind —for it is a grave omission—while we turn to the Majority Judgement's finding that Shigemitsu ' deliberately and recklessly disregarded his legal duty '.

" The words, ' deliberately and recklessly ' have puzzled many people.   There is no evidence to support them and there is evidence against them. . . .

Shigemitsu's Legal and Moral Responsibilities

" What was his legal duty ?   It was what was left over from Tojo.   It is not disputed that under Japanese law this was limited to receiving and passing on complaints on prisoner of war camps to the responsible department and to obtaining, if he could, their replies and passing them on to the complainant. That was his official duty. There is no suggestion that he failed in this respect. But the answers from the Department were always slow ; often they never came at all ; and they were rarely satisfactory. Perhaps some allowance should be made for the fact that a large proportion of the complaints related to camps in distant Islands, spread all over the Pacific, which as the war proceeded became more and more inaccessible. Even in a country like Great Britain, highly organized as it is, extraordinary mistakes can be made. It took me over two years to secure the release of a family of German Jews who were proved in the end to be absolutely and completely innocent. There were two brothers, one of whom was sent to Australia and the other to the Isle of Man. The wife of the Isle of Man brother was sent to Australia, and the wife of the Australian brother was sent to the Isle of Man. And the poor mother-in-law or grandmother (I forget which), who was a very strict vegetarian, died of a wrong diet before anything could be done. A matter like that can take two years, even in this country; and I have heard of a great many other cases. One cannot be surprised, therefore, if these prisoner of war cases took some time, in a war that was spread all over the high seas.

" The Tribunal, however, say that Shigemitsu had also legal responsibility as a member of the Government. The word ' legal ' seems arguable ; but, anyway, as a diplomat with Western experience, he had, of course, a moral responsibility to do all that he could—and he would be the last man to neglect it. To begin with, we must bear in mind that before he could get anyone to listen to him he had to secure some confirmation of the alleged facts, which the responsible military authorities would obviously seek to belittle. He had no time and no authority to visit the camps, either in Japan or in the distant islands, or to send anyone to check the allegations. He was entirely in the hands of the military authorities, and especially of Tojo, who alone had the knowledge, the means of obtaining knowledge, the power to issue orders and the decision.

Shigemitsu's Efforts for Redress

" Yet Shigemitsu was much more active than the majority finding led us to believe. Mr. Justice Roling's dissenting judgement, though it is not in the Majority Judgement, states that 'he complained to Kido'—that is, the Emperor's adviser—'that the military were not easy to deal with regarding these matters, and on some occasions personally approached the War Minister on the subject.' Undoubtedly the approaches to Kido were intended to be, and probably were, passed to the Emperor. I do not know what passed between him and Tojo, but we can all imagine it. Nothing of that appears in the majority finding. The Majority Judgement on all the prisoners, however, showed that occasionally he secured promises of concessions, which he passed on—only to find they were never implemented.

"After Tojo's retirement in July, 1944, Shigemitsu took an even more important step, which again is omitted from the finding in the Majority Judgement on Shigemitsu. To dig that out we have to turn back many pages to the judgement on Koiso, where we find 'that in October, 1944', that is, after Koiso had been Prime Minister less than two months, 'the Foreign Minister' who, of course, was Shigemitsu, though his name was not mentioned in the finding 'reported to a meeting of the Supreme Council for the Direction of War, which Koiso attended, that according to recent information from enemy sources it was reported that the Japanese treatment of prisoners of war left much to be desired.' That was the restrained way in which it was put. 'He further stated that this was a matter of importance from the point of view of Japan's international reputation and future relations. He asked that directions be issued to the competent authorities so that the matter could be fully discussed.'

"That reads like a soulless Cabinet summary, devised to avoid friction—of which, I fear, I have drafted many in my time—conveying nothing of the passion and drama that often weighs over such a scene. But the passage is of enormous importance to Shigemitsu's innocence, for it shows that he forced the question—no doubt against military opposition—to the highest military authority in the land. Yet it is completely ignored in the Shigemitsu findings of the Majority Judgement : there is not even a cross reference to it, and, as I have said, his name is omitted from the reference to him in the Koiso findings, where he is referred to only as 'the Foreign Minister'.

" I submit that, combined with the evidence I have already mentioned of what Shigemitsu did in Tojo's time, this evidence goes far to dispose of the statement in the majority findings that ' he took no adequate steps to have the matter investigated, although he, as a member of the Government, bore overhead responsibility for the welfare of the prisoners.' I do not know what more he could have done. He took steps to ensure that the Emperor knew what was going on. On occasions he went to the Prime Minister and eventually he took the question to the highest military authority in the country, the Supreme Council of War, which included the naval and military authorities responsible for prisoner of war camps.

" Mr. Furness, counsel for the defence, wrote a letter on December 10, 1948, which I have here. He said of Shigemitsu : ' He did many things which I could not bring out in evidence or in my petition.' He did say what the ' many things ', or some of the ' many things ', were, but, as Mr. Furness considered that his lips were sealed, I cannot mention the matter either. But I did inform the Lord Chancellor confidentially."

The Lord Chancellor (Viscount Jowitt) : " May I point out that the only reason why Mr. Furness could not say these things was that Mr. Shigemitsu declined to go into the witness box ? "

Lord Hankey : " The reason why Shigemitsu declined to go into the witness box, as I find from other letters, is that he was afraid of giving away other people—colleagues. The noble and learned Viscount on the Woolsack smiles. This is a man who has been in prison. It is exactly what I gather he would do. I know him quite well and I am perfectly certain that he would not give away a colleague. To me, that is something very admirable.

" The letter continues : ' I am certain that he had no knowledge. Civilians were not allowed to investigate ; but he was deeply disturbed by the protests he had received. It is admitted that any man who had served as a diplomat in Western countries would be disturbed. His power was limited to persuasion, to bringing the matter before the Supreme Council for the Direction of War, which he did, and to trying to end the war.' And, of course, to end the war was the one sure way of curing the trouble.

" The Tribunal says that Shigemitsu should have pressed the prisoners of war question to the point of resignation, if necessary. What good would that have done in a country like Japan ? In Japan, resignation would have been treated as a cowardly desertion of his country in time of war and would have prevented his pursuing his main object, to bring the war to an end. His efforts for peace failed : how could they succeed in view of our policy of Unconditional Surrender? Nevertheless a few months later, Shigemitsu, at the risk of his life—it was the second time he risked his life for peace—signed the surrender on behalf of the Emperor and the Government, which should stand him in good stead with His Majesty's Government. It is not mentioned in the findings of the majority, so far as I can discover."

None of these points were answered—to my mind they cannot be answered.

" I solemnly urge the Government, with all the force at my command, to make a great effort to secure the release of Mamoru Shigemitsu, so that he may become available once more to help his country on to sounder lines. I know the difficulties, but they are not insuperable. It cannot be that a body, whatever body it was, that can create a great international machinery like this for trials and sentences and for carrying out imprisonment, cannot devise some means of revision. Appeals for clemency were made to General MacArthur, but the time allowed for them was very short. The actual Judgement was published in a Japanese newspaper which I think appeared on December 13,[1] and only until December 19[1]—six days—was allowed for appeals. I myself signed a telegram, in company with Mr. R. A. Butler, Sir Robert Craigie, Sir Edward Crowe, Mr. Arthur Edwardes, Mr. H. A. Gwynne, Sir Francis Lindley, Major-General Francis Piggott, and Lord Sempill—there was no time to collect more names. But nothing came of it. It means an approach to all the nations, or at least to the majority that took part in the trials, which, after all means only ten approaches, including approaches to three Dominions and the countries of the three justices who entered dissents. But the solid fact remains that Shigemitsu is in American custody and it ought not to be impossible to secure his release and, I should

[1] The actual month was November.

hope, his reprieve. We ought to hammer away until we obtain it.

" I realize, of course, that I have made only a *prima facie* case, a layman's case at that, and that before they take action the Government have to satisfy themselves that it has some validity. It is not for me to suggest the precise machinery. I can only urge that it should be speedy and calculated to reassure public opinion. It should include persons with political as well as judicial experience. Shigemitsu should have the benefit of the doubt, if there is a doubt. Subject to this, my suggestions are as follows : first, speedy action to secure the release of Shige-mitsu ; second, a review of all the Tokyo sentences ; third, an end to the Japanese war crimes trials ; and fourth, as soon as practicable, an amnesty. I beg to move for Papers."

The Lord Chancellor's Reply

After my speech the Debate fell for a short time into some confusion as Lord Oaksey and the Earl of Perth, who had not been able to reply to my speech on the German Trials a fort-night before, wanted to come back to them to make some important observations which were discussed in Chapter Five. The Earl of Perth, however, supported my appeal for a revision of Shigemitsu's sentence. After Lord Justice Wright had ob-jectively dealt with some of the legal and organizational aspects of both trials Lord Sempill gave spirited support to my appeal for Shigemitsu in the course of which he gave a short message, in the same strain, from Lord Killearn, who had had to leave for the Far East on the previous day. Lord Winster followed with a thoughtful and moderate speech in general support of a re-examination of Shigemitsu's case.

Then the Lord Chancellor replied for the Government. One surprising point which emerged was this : apart from the review by the Supreme Commander, General MacArthur, who would consult the diplomatic representatives of the various Powers concerned—a review which had actually allowed only about a week for the preparation of petitions—*the Charter provided for no other review at all.* New evidence might come to light ; public opinion in the victor countries might totally change, as probably it will ; but there is no machinery for review ! To the layman that suggests lack of prescience. It

must increase the misgivings caused by the procedure adopted
so far.

If, however, the Lord Chancellor had felt that injustice had
been done, or even that there was a grave risk that injustice
had been done, he made it clear that he would not hesitate to
take steps so that a rehearing or another review might take
place. But he could see no reason to doubt the fairness of the
trial or the accuracy of the conclusions. He flatly declined to
take any action at all. In doing so he referred hardly to
the details of the case made by any of the speakers who had
urged revision. All he did in this respect was to give the controversial interpretation of just 'one telegram' and to remark on
the findings of the Majority Judgement on waging aggressive war.

On the question of Prisoners of War he devoted most of his
speech to an impassioned, sensational, and heart-rending account
of the Japanese atrocities in some of the prisoner of war and
interned civilian camps. This no one had questioned. Everyone deplored them as deeply as he did. What had this to do
with my charge that an innocent man had been adjudged
wrongly? Politically, however, it was a brilliant tactical move.
It captured most of the publicity to the exclusion of the criticism of the trials. In a torrent of rhetoric the Lord Chancellor
entirely overlooked what had been said in the Debate about
the concentration of responsibility—on P.O.W. matters for
policy, day-to-day control, and answers to the complaints of
the Powers—in Tojo and his successor Koiso and the naval
and military authorities, who were completely independent and
resented civilian interference. It was they who committed
the crimes. He did not hint at the severe limitation on Shigemitsu's responsibilities, which made the Japanese Foreign
Office little more than a Post Office for receiving complaints,
passing them on to the P.O.W. organization, where they were
dealt with at the bi-weekly meetings of Tojo's own Committee,
and passing on that Committee's replies.

Among errors and omissions the Lord Chancellor, in saying
that time after time Shigemitsu refused the demands of
the Swiss Minister (who represented the Protecting Power) to
exercise his right of inspection, omitted to mention that
Shigemitsu could only pass on the decisions of Tojo's organization. He impeached Shigemitsu for 'refusing' to allow

inspection—as though he had unlimited authority in this matter, when, as a matter of fact he had none ! He made no mention at all of the efforts that Shigemitsu did nevertheless make, not even of the fact that he forced the matter before the highest tribunal in the land—the Supreme Council of War. In fact, he tried to saddle this civilian Foreign Minister—new to office at that— with all the crimes which the Majority Judgement had laid fairly and squarely on Tojo and Koiso.

At the end of his speech, after having spoken not long before of Shigemitsu as ' knowing that these things were going on' the Lord Chancellor refused to review the sentences, *because he believed ' that if he had made an inspection it would have revealed these horrible things '*. Lord Jowitt cannot have it both ways. On reflection he must see that his statements were self-contradictory. What use would it have been for the Foreign Minister to inspect what he already knew ? But it does not seem to have occurred to Viscount Jowitt that, in order to visit a camp, Shigemitsu (or his nominee) would have had to obtain a pass from Tojo's P.O.W. Department, who were in complete control and resented civilian interference; that, if he had succeeded, under Japanese military regulations, he would have been accompanied by an escort who would not have allowed him to see more than they wished ; and that he would only have been permitted to visit camps which had been purged of everything objectionable —as happened to the neutral observers who, through Shigemitsu's good offices (a fact not mentioned by the Lord Chancellor), were sometimes permitted to pay such visits. But Shigemitsu, like the Swiss Minister, would never have been allowed to visit the camps in the vast southern area of the Pacific where the worst crimes were committed and where, according to a statement by Mr. Eden on January 28, 1944, eighty to ninety per cent of the camps were situated. Given the disorganization of Japan's overseas communications in the last year of the war that would, in any event, have been impossible for this one-legged Foreign Minister, even if he could have been spared.

The Lord Chancellor, of course, had the task to defend these trials. He is so able a man—and so brilliant an advocate, that I am certain no better case could have been made than was, in fact, put forward by him. Yet, it avoided many points mentioned on behalf of Shigemitsu, and was not convincing.

More than eloquence, and what a splendid speaker Lord Jowitt is! is necessary to remove the misgivings so many people have about these trials.

The End of the Japanese War Crimes Trials

Only on one point did the Lord Chancellor give complete satisfaction, namely, when he announced that the Far Eastern Commission decided on February 24, 1949, that there shall be no further international tribunals and recommended that the investigation of minor war crimes should be completed by the end of June, 1949.

Conclusion

What Shigemitsu's friends are asking for is nothing unreasonable. The Tribunal itself gave him much the lightest sentence of any of the condemned and explained its comparative leniency as follows :—' In mitigation of sentence we take into account that Shigemitsu was in no way involved in the formulation of the conspiracy ; that he waged no war of aggression until he became Foreign Minister in April, 1943, by which time his country was deeply involved in a war which would vitally affect its future ; and in the matter of war crimes, that the military completely controlled Japan while he was Foreign Minister so that it would have required great resolution for any Japanese to condemn them.'

All that is now asked is this : having already served more than half his sentence, this man, to whose character so many striking tributes have been rendered by his former enemies, should have the remainder remitted. Some of us think it should be remitted altogether, but *bis dat qui cito dat*, and personally I should advocate the quickest method by which the cumbrous and unorganized procedure of international effort in such matters can be made to work.

This is not solely a question of justice—and who could claim that there is too much of it in the world ?—nor even of mercy : and again peacemaking without mercy is an impossibility. There is also a question of policy. Even on a short view it is desirable that a man of Shigemitsu's abilities should be available to assist in his country's rehabilitation. And whenever this comes about, as it surely will—provided he survives his sentence—he should not come to the task embittered against Great Britain and America. In that connection the following extract from a letter dated December 10, 1948, from Mr. Furness to Major-General Francis Piggott (which I have permission to use) is revealing : ' I hope,' the Counsel writes, ' His friends in England will think no less of him, for he is still the same charming and sensitive man that you knew in London and in Japan. He is wise, far-seeing and generous and still without bitterness. The tragic aspect of the whole thing is that he is not free to take his part in Japan's reconstruction. . . . The broad statesmanship of a man like Mr. Shigemitsu . . . is needed now more than ever before.' Looking still further ahead we do not want to make more martyrs than necessary : and Shigemitsu is of the stuff of which martyrs are made.

CHAPTER SEVEN

THE AFTERMATH OF TOKYO

THE judges having spoken at Nuremberg and at Tokyo, what else is there to be said? In an ordinary trial all ends there. But these political trials, as we have seen, were not only wrongly conceived and wrongly executed ; they have created new and bigger problems than they set out to solve. Before casting up this balance sheet, however, we can with profit, go still deeper into the sheer inexhaustible material provided by the Tokyo Judgements themselves. Moreover, an increasing amount of information has reached me since from Japan direct. Obviously matters cannot be allowed to rest where the Debate which I initiated in the House of Lords, left them. Mr. Shigemitsu, himself deeply moved by the efforts of his British and American friends, sent me a message from his prison cell : surely, justice must be done. The stone-walling in which the spokesman of His Majesty's Government indulged, cannot be the last word. I also received numerous statements from American, British and other European citizens, who urged me to continue demanding a reversal of the policy of revenge carried out so far under the cloak of a trial.

The Protest of the Defence Counsel

Whereas no allied lawyers were allowed to assist the defence at Nuremberg, a small but devoted group of American jurists were sent by the United States Government to help the defendants at Tokyo. This act of mercy will long be remembered in Japan, for they have given of their best and have fought and are fighting their hardest for their clients. Legal experts might argue that their work was not mercy but a necessary part of any real trial : if so I wonder how they would explain the absence of such counsel at Nuremberg.

Only one member of that group, Mr. George Furness, was known to me personally. In addition, Mr. Ben Bruce Blakeney, the *doyen* of the group, has spontaneously sent me further

111

information. The reader will want to see some of this additional voluminous material for himself—if doubts could still lurk in any reader's mind as to whether the Tokyo Tribunal was one which could be relied on to give a fair trial to enemy prisoners! The following memorial on the conduct of the trial was presented on November 21, 1948 (shortly after the close of the trial), to General MacArthur, Supreme Commander for the Allied Powers, *on behalf of the whole group* of Defence Counsel at the Trials. I print it here with the permission of the *doyen* of the group who signed the memorandum on their behalf. The reader will notice that many of its criticisms are in line with passages in the dissenting reports of judges:

November, 21 1948.

To the Supreme Commander for the Allied Powers :

' Availing themselves of permission granted, defence counsel for all defendants convicted by the International Military Tribunal for the Far East present this memorandum of points of general applicability. These points have all been treated more fully in the petitions filed on behalf of the defendants individually ; here we attempt in the briefest possible compass to sum up the general principles involved.

The Trial was Unfair

'The prosecution did not present its case fairly ; the Tribunal did not allow the defendants a fair trial. The Chief Prosecutor is reported by the press as having admitted that he prosecuted defendants who were " felt to be of the same mind as us of the United States "—but they were prosecuted, and the death penalty was demanded for all. The Tribunal established rules of procedure for the prosecution, changed them and made them more strict when the defence was being presented, and changed them back again when the prosecution's evidence in rebuttal was offered. The Tribunal refused to hear certain defences which were pleaded, but in its verdict says that those defences cannot be sustained " because there is no evidence to support " them. The Tribunal accepted from the prosecution "evidence" in the form of newspaper reports, second and third-hand rumours and hearsay, opinions of self-styled "experts", and made its findings and verdict on the basis of such " evidence " ; it ignored all defence evidence in its verdict, saying that the evidence of Japanese witnesses (although not those who testified for the prosecution) was unsatisfactory and unreliable.

' Judges of the Tribunal, in dissenting opinions, have pointed out the unfairness of the proceedings. Mr. Justice Bernard of France, says that " the dispositions of the Charter approved . . . by the Supreme Commander for the Allied Powers, super-abundantly manifest their desire to assure the Defendants the maximum guarantees possible. . . . Though I am of opinion that the Charter permitted granting to the accused guarantees sufficient for their defence, I think that actually these were not granted to them " ; and he gives concrete examples. Mr. Justice Roling, of The Netherlands, points out instance after instance in which the Tribunal has unfairly construed the evidence, or even ignored it or made findings in the teeth of it. Mr. Justice Pal, of India, has devoted seventy pages of his opinion to the demonstration of the exact way in which the Tribunal's method of procedure and rulings crippled the defence. The President of the Tribunal admits that there was, when the last war started, and is now, much doubt whether aggressive war is a crime.

The Verdict is Not Based on the Evidence

' The verdict has been plainly stated by some judges of the Tribunal not to have been based on the evidence ; Mr. Justice Bernard has said that he is unable to deny or affirm " that all the evidence and only the evidence produced during the course of the trial was taken into consideration ", or that " the points of law and findings of facts adopted by the majority were done so outside of all assistance of persons other than judges ". Not only does the verdict give no indication that any of the evidence produced by the defence was taken into consideration, but the great mass of evidence from prosecution witnesses and documents favourable to defendants is never acknowledged ; the entire verdict is in the tone of a prosecution's summation, with no favourable reference to any defendant ever admitted. One judge of the majority, who wrote a special opinion to express his insistence on still harsher verdicts, almost confesses his lack

I

of interest in the evidence when he thrice quotes, and emphasizes, the words of the Charter providing for " trial and *punishment* " of the defendants. Not even of those defendants convicted by a bare majority, and given the rare light sentences, is there a good word in the majority verdict.

Guilt has not been Proved beyond a Reasonable Doubt

' The verdict is not that of the Tribunal, but of a clique of it. It has been disclosed that the seven-judge majority excluded from the deliberations and decision not only Messrs. Justices Pal and Bernard, who dissented generally, but Mr. Justice Roling who dissented in part and concurred in part, and the President, Sir William Webb, who expressed grave doubts concerning several points of the result, but recorded no dissent. It is known that death sentences were imposed by vote of six to five in some cases, of seven to four in others, but in no case by vote of more than seven judges. The law of most of the civilized world requires unanimity for imposing a sentence of death, and usually for conviction of a crime ; we Americans would consider it an outrage that six or seven men out of eleven should convict and sentence to death, and the community of civilized nations must regard it as an outrage here. Guilt has not been proved beyond a reasonable doubt, but the " doubt " in some cases is so overwhelming that there cannot even be said to be a reasonable doubt of guilt.

The Verdict will not achieve the Allied Powers' Purposes

' The purposes of our nations in holding these trials are two ; to establish it as the law that aggression is a crime, to be paid for by heavy penalties ; and to impress upon our defeated enemies and the world, that our attachment to the law which we are acting in support of is such that we will accord even those enemies a fair trial by judicial process. This verdict must inevitably fail to further either end.

' The state of the international law relating to crimes against peace is not clarified, but muddled, by this verdict. The Tribunal produced six separate opinions, from consideration of all of which it is impossible for even an international lawyer to determine what law is being applied. Not only dissenting judges, but judges concurring in the result, have written opinions expressing grave doubts concerning some of the doctrines adopted by the majority, which doctrines in such cases may prove to be those of only a plurality even of this Tribunal ; such doctrines as do rest on a clear majority will have little influence on international law, which is based on the concensus of all or an overwhelming majority of civilized nations. If the trial of the military and civilian leaders of defeated nations is to be a normal aftermath of war, for the sake of all of us we had better see to the establishment of definitely fixed law under which to punish them.

' The verdict looks too much like an act of vengeance to impress the world with our love of justice and fair play. The conviction of all defendants alike, even those whom the prosecution admits should not have been charged and of those whose conviction they are " ashamed " compares unfavourably with the result of the Nuremberg trial, where guilt or innocence, as well as sentence, were declared individually rather than *en masse*—even though, as the President of our Tribunal has pointed out, " the crimes of the German accused were far more heinous, varied and extensive than those of the Japanese accused ". This verdict looks too much like vindictiveness to impress the Japanese people, who see convicted, all alike, statesmen who were notorious in militaristic Japan for fighting for peace, soldiers who merely entered a war late, men who voiced outspoken opposition to aggression, or who at great risks worked to end the war.

' And, lastly, as to the effect on ourselves—for we who address you are Americans, and if this trial was international, the Supreme Commander whose action is now awaited is an American, and his act will be considered that of America. We can only stultify ourselves if we become party to the use of the forms of law and justice to perpetrate acts of vengeance. We will not impress our enemies ; we will not gain the respect of our friends ; we will in the end brutalize and destroy ourselves. A hundred and fifty years ago Lord Erskine—that impassioned defender of justice and liberty whose name has outlasted those of all the prosecutors whom he met in the arena—in one of his celebrated defences, speaking of England, put the matter in terms equally applicable to the international community whose course is here involved, and in words of equal significance for our day : " Unjust prosecutions lead to the ruin of all governments. Whoever will look back to the history of the world in general, and of our own particular country, will be convinced that exactly as prosecutions have been cruel and oppressive, and maintained by inadequate and unrighteous evidence, in the same proportion, and by the same means, their authors have been destroyed instead of being supported by them. As often as the principles of our ancient laws have been departed from in weak and wicked times, so often have the governments that have violated them been suddenly crumbled into dust."

' If we hope for a world organized under law and operating under the rule of law and the principles of justice, we must not ourselves be guilty of atrocities against the law and justice. No good, but only pyramided evil, will come from the verdict of this Tribunal as it now stands. A fearless act of statesmanship now can salvage much of the prestige which the act of this small group of judges would lose to our countries : we urge that it be performed.

> *Ben Bruce Blakeney,*
> *On behalf of all Defence Counsel.'*

This Memorandum provides a remarkable commentary, so far as the Tokyo trials are concerned, on Lord Wright's defence in the House of Lord's debate on May 19, of trials by the victors of the vanquished. This criticism, Lord Wright considered, was unfair and irrelevant. In his view the only proper questions were : ' Did the men have a fair trial ? Were the facts properly put before the court ; and did the court impartially come to the best view it could ? '[1] Each of these three pertinent questions is answered in the negative in this Memorandum by American Counsel for the defendants. It says in so many words that ' the trial was unfair ' ; that ' the prosecution did not present its case fairly ; ' and that ' the Tribunal did not allow the defendants a fair trial '. By these experts, who had given their mind to these trials for month after month, all three of Lord Justice Wright's test questions were anticipated and answered in the negative. And in each case they gave, what appeared to

---

[1] *Hansard,* House of Lords, May 19, 1949, Col. 887.

be solid and convincing reasons for their criticisms, which, of course, go far beyond Lord Wright's questions. Not only that, but they cite in their support several of the eleven judges.

It is rather curious that in his speech Lord Wright, after explaining the many difficulties of trying—through interpreters—Japanese on questions of law, diplomacy, and commerce, gave among other reasons for the length of the Tokyo trial the following : ' If I may say so, without any responsibility for it, I think a good deal of delay was caused by the well-meaning act of the United States Government in sending out from the United States one American counsel to act for each of the defendants. Perhaps it may not appear strange that that did not tend to expedition in the course of the trial. But it was well meant, and I hope it was fully appreciated by the beneficiaries '.

I am in a position to assure Lord Wright that their services are most deeply appreciated in the case of at least two beneficiaries who owe their lives to these defending Counsel. In the only case with which I am closely familiar Counsel never hesitated to undertake long and dangerous journeys at the worst seasons of the year on behalf of his clients, and no one can read their pleas without realizing that they compare very favourably with other documents in the case, including the Majority Judgement.

To see the case in its proper perspective the reader will want to have these further commentaries, sent spontaneously by Counsel for the Defence, on Lord Wright's remarks : ' The well-meaning act of the United States Government in providing American counsel was an act performed upon the written representation of the Acting President of the Tribunal, Mr. Justice (now Sir Erima) Northcroft of New Zealand, that it was necessary to a fair trial. American counsel were not provided " one . . . to act for each of the defendants " ; several of us, myself included, carried two cases throughout the proceedings. We can, doubtless, agree to Lord Wright's point that the proceedings would have been more expeditious if the making of a defence had not been permitted, but hardly to the implication that it was therefore naïve or foolish to permit it. Finally, his suggestion that it was the presence of American defence counsel to which the length of the proceedings was attributable is not only without foundation in fact but is a gratuitous reflection upon the only branch of the Tribunal which, I venture to say, will come off with credit when the verdict of history is in.'

The reasons for the length of the proceedings, in the view of the defence counsel, were very different indeed : (i) The length of the ' indictment ' drawn up by the prosecution and approved by the Tribunal, which ran to fifty-five counts and included every grievance, going back to the—originally Allied—Siberian expedition of 1918–22. (ii) The Tribunal's admission of any ' evidence', no matter how flimsy or preposterous, offered by the prosecution, all of which had to be met by the defence. (iii) The disinclination of the majority of the judges to work. The verdict (which, as I, myself, pointed out in my speech on May 19, suggested that they had not co-ordinated the evidence) required six months—one fourth of the trial. (iv) The difficulty of attaining even a satisfactory approximation of accuracy in translation between the English and Japanese languages. (v) The wasting of time by defence counsel (chiefly Japanese unfamiliarity with our procedure) and by prosecuting counsel (not Japanese).

Personally I have not criticized the length of the trial, because long experience of international co-operation in other fields has taught me how slow and unsatisfactory and inefficient it always is. But Lord Wright's reflection on the value of the American Defence Counsel had to be mentioned here because I have seen sufficient of their work to realize how valuable it has been as an attempt to right the balance so heavily loaded against the defendants. The very suggestion that they were superfluous in a trial beset with well-nigh insuperable difficulties is a gift to those who are saying that these were mock trials to obtain a conviction, which had been settled beforehand. It must certainly increase the doubts of those like myself who think that these trials were not of the high quality that is imperative when the lives of human beings are at stake. And the defendants included experienced statesmen, friends of the United Kingdom and the United States, and former workers for peace.

At any rate, putting the value of their work at its lowest for purposes of argument, the presence of these counsel was indispensable to give the impression of a fair trial, especially after the Acting President's statement that it was necessary for that purpose. To quote the passage from ' the classic language of Lord Hewart, Lord Chief Justice of England' (which is part of our tradition) : 'It is not only of some importance, but it is of fundamental importance that justice should not only be done but should manifestly and openly be seen to be done.' To have rejected or opposed the presence of these distinguished men who gave such yeoman service, would have been a deplorable blunder. Even to hint at their exclusion gives the impression that we wanted a trial that was not fair, and did not even appear fair ! But perhaps it was even a worse blunder, after bringing them in, to conduct the business in such a way as to provoke their scathing indictment of the trials. True, no man is a hero to his valet. And counsel are the valets to the Court. They always know what is going on ; but there must have been a good deal amiss to provoke such a formidable protest as that contained in their Memorandum to General MacArthur.

What makes their words ring true is the fact that much support for their views comes also from the Minority Judgements.

But probably the end of the fifth paragraph of the Memorandum gave to my fellow countrymen and readers in the United States as nasty a jolt as it did to me ; the words : ' The law of most of the civilized world requires unanimity for imposing a sentence of death, and usually for conviction for a crime ; we Americans would consider it an outrage that six or seven men out of eleven should convict and sentence to death, and the community of civilized nations must regard it as an outrage here.' It is sickening to think that this oddly assorted Court, with all its dissensions and faulty procedure could, and did *by majority*, sentence men to death and to long terms of imprisonment !

The case for the reprieve or remission of sentence on Shigemitsu has already been made. I have also read since the key documents in the case of Shigenori Togo—the verdict and sentence, the Majority and Minority Judgements, Counsel's case and his plea for mercy. But I have not been able to go into it in the same detail, nor have I the same personal acquaintance with Togo as with Shigemitsu. Study of the documents, however, reveals points of similarity between the two cases. Both occupied the post of Foreign Minister of Japan for relatively short periods. Both were lifelong workers for peace. Both were opposed to an Alliance with the European Axis. Both openly opposed the military party. Both were exonerated in the dissenting opinions. Togo, at the risk of his life, brought the war to an end ; and Shigemitsu, at the risk of his life, signed the surrender. The case of Togo, therefore, should unquestionably be added to the case of Shigemitsu for review with the highest priority. Naturally, this must not be taken to imply that the cases of the other survivors should not also be reviewed as soon as possible.

A revision of all of these cases will assuredly come in due course. But it will not come until public opinion in Britain and America insists that the weights of hate and vengeance shall be removed from the scales of justice, and replaced by mercy and forgiveness.

Relations with Japan—Revision

These are matters of policy every bit as much as they are matters of law. We have to live in the future with the Japanese, who hitherto have been the most go-ahead nation in Asia and will, before long, resume that position. In the past we did not find it difficult to live in peace and friendship with them. We did not denounce them or boycott them owing to their naval aggressions in 1894 and 1904. Those were the days when nations did not interfere in other nation's squabbles if they could help it, days when it was possible to ' ring round ' a war, even between great Powers, so as to prevent its becoming a world war. On the contrary, we made a Treaty of Alliance with Japan which was honourably fulfilled on both sides and which, to my personal knowledge, enabled us to avoid vast expenditure on dockyards and defences in the Far East. So long as that Alliance lasted, that is to say until 1922, we were able to talk plainly and on the dead level to Japan and, within limits, to restrain her from violent actions. My American friends will forgive me if I say that it was a mistake for the United States to insist, in 1921, as a condition of a naval Treaty, that we should cancel the Treaty with Japan. As both we and the Japanese delegates foresaw, the result was that our friends in Japan ' lost face ', our influence faded away, and eventually the military clique got control. *Hinc illæ lachrimæ.*

At the Washington Naval Conference, when the Sino–Japanese negotiations broke down and the Conference itself was in danger, I suggested to my ' opposite number ' Mr. Saburi, of precious memory, that they should try again, with ' solicitors ' —Mr. Hughes, with a deputy, as ' solicitor ' for China, and Mr. Balfour with a deputy (Mr. Miles Lampson, now Lord Killearn) for Japan, and that whenever they got in a jam the good offices of the ' solicitors ' should be sought. Saburi burst out laughing at this proposal, but the plan was adopted, succeeded admirably and was kept a complete secret. That shows the pattern of future relationship that we had in mind : and we had other equally close contacts at Washington with the American and Japanese delegations through Admiral (now Lord) Chatfield for the Navy, Colonel (now Major-General) Francis Piggott for the army, and so on. We were all of us out, as a team, to work closely with the Americans and the Japanese. If the Anglo-Japanese Alliance had only been maintained, history might have been different. People like our own Ambassadors, Sir Francis Lindley or Sir Robert Craigie, and the American Ambassador, Mr. Joseph Grew, might then have had a chance of success.

This illustrates the truth that there, as in other parts of the world, the decisive events which poisoned the nineteen-thirties, often took place in the nineteen-twenties—a point which even most historians overlook. A bilateral Treaty like that, which had proved its value, is a precious thing and worth a hundred multilateral Treaties that in the past have rarely stood up to a serious test.

To-day the United States, the temporary guardians of Japan, quite properly have the lead in that country, which is obviously their right and privilege. They shared with ourselves and the Dominions most of the responsibility for initiating the Tokyo Tribunal ; apart from that they have set an admirable example by sending the defence counsel, by helping the re-establishment of trade and industry and other liberal and enlightened acts of policy. They have also established in Washington in 1948 ' The American Council on Japan ', with which are associated Mr. Joseph Grew, Mr. Wm. Castle, and Mr. Harry F. Kern, Foreign Editor of *Newsweek*, so as to focus public attention on to the problem of American relations with Japan. There is a good deal to be said for the establishment of a companion body in this country, possibly a revival of the old Japan Society of London, which would have to work in close touch with the American Council and the Dominions.

If, between them, they could secure the release of Mr. Shige-mitsu and Mr. Togo, and a review of the sentences, they would make at least a start towards removing the dangerous con-sequences of unconditional surrender and the war crimes trials. A good deal more though would be required.

My correspondents in Japan are critical of the Lord Chan-cellor's statement in the House of Lords about the difficulties of reviewing sentences. It will be remembered that Viscount Jowitt's words were : ' The Charter provides for a review by the Supreme Commander who, of course, would consult (and this is so provided) with diplomatic representatives of the various Powers. That Charter provided for no other form of review at all. In fact the Supreme Commander did review these trials, awaiting for that purpose representations from all the various countries concerned.' This, according to my corre-spondents, contains several inaccuracies : Art. 17 of the Charter states that : ' The judgement will be announced in open court and will state the reasons on which it is based. *The record of the trial will be transmitted directly to the Supreme Com-mander for the Allied Powers for his action.*[1] Sentence will be carried out in accordance with the Order of the Supreme Com-mander for the Allied Powers, who may *at any time* reduce or otherwise alter the sentence, except to increase its severity.' There is thus no provision in the Charter for consultation with the Allied diplomatic representatives. This was provided by a ' policy decision ' of the Far Eastern Commission dated April 3, 1946, which was classified as ' Top Secret ' until long after the trial was under way.

The Lord Chancellor's statement continued : ' In fact, the Supreme Commander did review these trials, awaiting for that purpose representation from all the various countries con-cerned, and he confirmed the decision *in toto*.' The actual facts are reported by one of my correspondents to be as follows : ' A meeting was called of those diplomatic representatives on November 24—five days after the petitions for review were

---

[1] Author's italics.

filed, twelve days after announcement of the sentences—and they met with General MacArthur. Any "consultations" with the diplomatic representatives could only be nominal ; they could not make " representations ". No one of them had had instructions from his Government, indeed not one of those Governments had had opportunity to receive (far less to read) the judgement ; no one of them had had opportunity to see all the dissenting opinions, some of which were not yet then printed. These are facts known to me, for in the interim between verdict and " consultation " I discussed the situation personally with the chiefs of three, and members of two more diplomatic missions. I know that two of these chiefs expressed some doubts at the meeting on November 24; but none could speak under instructions. This was the " consultation "; the verdict, as the Lord Chancellor says, was confirmed " *in toto* ".'

This would explain unofficial reports from Tokyo according to which the British representative at the ' consultation ' did not take an active part. It does not seem likely that His Majesty's Government could have sent instructions until they had received the actual text of the Judgement. In that case the representative could not say much. What does seem extraordinary is that the death sentences should have been carried out without enabling the Nations concerned to engage in proper consultations. The implications of the Lord Chancellor's statement ' that the Supreme Commander did review these trials, awaiting representations from all the various countries concerned ' are in any case not borne out by my correspondent in Tokyo.

What of the Lord Chancellor's statement that, apart from the ' consultation ' ' no further review is possible. . . .' My correspondent on the spot rejects this altogether, and says : ' He overlooks the express language of the Charter of the Tribunal, that the Supreme Commander " may *at any time* reduce or otherwise alter the sentence ". It is to be presumed, in view of this provision, that upon suggestion by the Far Eastern Commission, or strong representation from some Allied Power or Powers, the Supreme Commander might well, if circumstances were favourable, undertake further review of the sentences.' I earnestly hope that this suggestion will be followed up, not only in the interests of justice and mercy but also of Britain's and America's future relations with Japan.

CHAPTER EIGHT

THE PAST, THE PRESENT, AND THE FUTURE

ALL along in this book I have been concerned with bringing to light the grave mistakes made by the Allies in their dealings with the former enemy—from the damage done by the policy of unconditional surrender to the revengeful trials and the Errors of Judgement, in every sense of those words! There has, of course, been no attempt to underrate, much less to condone the aggressions and war crimes of the enemy, but a dispassionate examination of the history of those times has revealed that the Russians in full measure, and we ourselves and other Allies in different degrees carried out operations which, by Nuremberg and Tokyo standards would render us liable to similar prosecutions. The omission from the judgements of any reference to such operations has been heavily criticized, and it has been suggested that the defence was gravely handicapped by the fact that evidence of that kind was not allowed.

The following episode is of peculiar interest and illustrates the difference which greater freedom to the defence to raise such matters actually made in one of the subsidiary trials.

Captain Russell Grenfell's ' Aggression '

In the spring of 1948 Captain Russell Grenfell, R.N., agreed to give evidence, as a naval historian and writer on strategical matters, at the trial of General-Admiral Schniewind, who, with Field-Marshal Sperrle and eleven German Generals, was being charged before an American Court at Nuremberg (Trial No. 12) with planning, preparing, and initiating aggressive warfare. The purport of Captain Russell Grenfell's evidence was that the dictionary defined " aggression " as in terms of action, the determining factor being whether the action was the first of its kind—the man who gets his blow in first is the aggressor.[1] On that basis, said Captain Grenfell, and since planning necessarily precedes action, there could be no such

[1] The Court being American, Captain Grenfell referred to Webster's dictionary.

thing as aggressive planning; it being impossible for the planners, as such, to know whether their plan would be used aggressively or not.

Captain Grenfell illustrated this argument by recalling that he himself had taken part in planning the Allied attack on French North Africa (with which, as he mentioned, his country was not at war), the invasion of which might conceivably have been carried out by the Axis forces before the Anglo-American landings took place. But as the Allies moved first, it followed that, if Admiral Schniewind was found guilty, Captain Grenfell ought logically to be put into the dock as well.

That seems to have gone home. The General-Admiral, the Field-Marshal and all the Generals were acquitted on Count I, Crimes against peace, on the ground that they were below the policy making level and therefore not guilty of planning, preparing, or initiating aggressive war.

The sequel was even more remarkable. A later Court in the so-called " Foreign Office " case (Case 11) found von Weizsäcker, Keppler, Woermann, and Lammers guilty under Count I, Crimes against Peace, of planning aggressive war after the Admiral and the Generals had been acquited of it. The General-Admiral, the Field-Marshal, and the Generals were adjudged below the policy making level in planning preparing or in initiating war and therefore not guilty. But the Civil Servants were judged to be above the line and therefore guilty. And that was the judgement of a so-called Military Tribunal! But it is only fair to record that one of the American judges (*Times*, April 14, 1949) dissented.

I am indebted to Captain Russell Grenfell, R.N., for the above account.

The Balance Sheet

To cast up the balance sheet I should perhaps first of all summarize my indictment and list the mistakes.

Unconditional Surrender and War Crimes Trials have been denounced as complementary parts of a policy of threats which was adopted in 1943, and has exercised the most sinister and far reaching influence ever since. It embittered the war, rendered inevitable a fight to a finish, banged the door to any possibility of either side offering terms or opening up negotiations, gave the Germans and Japanese the courage of despair, strengthened Hitler's position as Germany's ' only hope ', aided Goebbels's propaganda, and made inevitable the Normandy landing and the subsequent terribly exhausting and destructive advance through North France, Belgium, Luxemburg, Holland and Germany.[1] The lengthening of the war enabled Stalin to occupy the whole of eastern Europe, to ring down the iron curtain and so to realize at one swoop a large instalmemt of his avowed aims against so-called capitalism, in which he includes social democracy. By disposing of all the more competent administrators in Germany and Japan this policy rendered treaty-making impossible after the war and retarded recovery and reconstruction, not only in Germany and Japan, but everywhere else. It may also prove to have poisoned our future relations with ex-enemy countries. Not only the enemy countries, but nearly all countries were bled white by this policy, which has left us all, except the United States of America, impoverished and in dire straits. Unfortunately also, these policies, so contrary to the spirit of the Sermon on the Mount, did nothing to strengthen the moral position of the Allies.

To these criticisms of policy must be added the misgivings that are raised by the proceedings of the London Conference of June, 1945, where persons delegated as prosecutor or judge drafted the Charter for the Nuremberg Trial and discussed *inter alia* the desirability of excluding the raising at the trials of large issues of fact and policy, which captured documents had shown to be necessary to the defence. The actual exclusion of many such questions as irrelevant increases these misgivings. Other criticisms to which I shall revert presently, are the system of trials by Victors of the Vanquished, the creation *ad hoc* and *ex post facto* of new, so-called crimes, for which no one had ever been tried before, including aggression. In that connection another criticism (only touched upon before) must be discussed at greater length,

---

[1] In December, 1948, in Rotterdam I was shown two scenes of utter desolation. Of the first I was told that it was done by the Germans at the outset of the war : of the second, not far away, that it was done by the Allies in the liberation. Both had completely missed their targets in the port.

namely the ignoring by the Tribunals of the Russian aggressions, which took place simultaneously with the German aggressions of 1939–40, and the realization of the fruits of these acts after the war. The fatal bearing on the trials of ' Soviet Susceptibilities ' are also added in this Chapter to my indictment. Finally I must add a few points of criticism that have only recently come to notice—first, the absence of British Counsel for the Defence from both trials ; second the inordinate length of the indictments of the accused, which is said by some lawyers to be contrary to British practice and to have made it impossible for the defendants and their counsel to cover all the points adequately.

The Advantages Claimed

What are the ' advantages ' claimed for the trials by their defenders ? We must compare them with the, to my mind formidable, array of disadvantages marshalled so far. But even before listing them it is worth mentioning that few people go so far as to claim that the policies of Unconditional Surrender and War Crimes Trials are likely to stop future wars. Occasionally they might act as a deterrent to a very flagrant aggression ; but an adventurer like Hitler who has worked up the grievances of his people to a point where they consider that their only hope lies in a successful war is not likely to be deterred by the possibility of being tried by his enemies. Trials might however serve as a deterrent to the commission of conventional war crimes against prisoners of war, internees and so forth—but, as already mentioned more than once, that is not the subject of this book.

One of the most comprehensive lists of the advantages claimed is given in a Report on the Nuremberg Trials sent by the American Chief Prosecutor to the President of the United States of America on October 7, 1945.[1] First in the list of accomplishments is put the Charter itself, and its adoption by adherence of nineteen nations. No one will grudge praise to those who reached agreement in such difficult conditions in June, 1945, and the London Conference was notable as one of the rare occasions since the end of the war in Europe when agreement has been reached between representatives of the

[1] Paper LXIII of State Department publication on the London Conference, June, 1945.

Western Powers and Russia on an important issue. Yet, can the reader of these proceedings—summarized above in Chapter One, escape misgivings ? The Chief Prosecutors Designate at the coming trial were then acting as a drafting Committee to settle the rules of the Tribunal. There is no doubt that the Charter is popular in some high judicial circles ; but some distinguished legal authorities, both in England and America, are not enamoured by these trials at all, and among them are even prosecutors at some of the lesser trials both in Germany and Japan. As we saw in the last Chapter the defending counsel at the Tokyo Tribunal made a joint protest to General MacArthur against the unfairness of the trials, which was to some extent a criticism of the Charter. There is very little, then, in the first claim.

The Chief Prosecutor's second advantage claimed is the incorporation in the principles of the Charter of the ' power of the precedent ' . If that means such precedents as trials of the Vanquished by the Victors, and the making—by the prosecutors designated for the trial—of new crimes *ex post facto*, and of rules to enable important evidence to be excluded, then a great many people will differ as to its being anything like a precedent of which we ought to be proud. If the ' precedent ' is set with a view to a universal practice by the Victor in every future war of setting up his own Tribunal with his own list of crimes to try and punish the leading politicians and Generals and thousands of the citizens of the vanquished as war criminals, then the outlook is stupefying.

The third claim—' a workable procedure for the trial of crimes surmounting international difficulties '—is a matter of opinion depending on the meaning of the word ' workable '. The system does not appear to have proved very ' workable ' at the Tokyo trials to judge from the dissenting judgements of Mr. Justice Roling, M. Bernard, and Mr. Pal.

The fourth claim is that in a world torn with hatreds ' the Four Powers have given the example of submitting their grievances against these men to a dispassionate inquiry on legal evidence '. Not everyone will agree that an inquiry undertaken exclusively by Victors can be described as ' dispassionate '.

The Chief Prosecutor's fifth claim is that Nazi aggressions, persecution, and other nefarious activities have, as the result of these trials, been so carefully docketed and documented that ' there can be no responsible denial of their crimes in the future and no tradition of martyrdom of the Nazi leaders can arise among informed people '. That might be worth something if the mass of the people were well informed. But they are not. After a generation has passed away who can say that the Germans will not be as gullible as they were in the nineteen-thirties ? It is unlikely that their history books will tell the school children what we think they ought to know, and it will be extremely difficult to get the Chief Prosecutor's lesson home to them. I wonder whether some such words were not said of Joan of Arc in May, 1431, when she was burned as a witch! But her crimes have been refuted and she is now a Saint and a Martyr. Moreover, the mistakes of the trials themselves have been ' docketed and documented ' in this book and others.

In Britain a frequent claim is that the trials have uprooted National Socialism and all its works. That is doubtful. For the Nazi system was based on that militarism that we thought to have destroyed by the victory of 1918, and the Versailles Treaty of 1919. Suppression, however, only forced it underground, and fifteen years later Germany was rearming and militarism was more rampant than ever. With Europe now divided into two camps, both striving for the body and soul of Germany no one can predict the result. But German civilization and culture are nearer to western than to eastern ideals, and one day her much decried militarism may become the pivot of western defence. Before then the Victor Powers should do their utmost to mitigate the results of unconditional surrender and war crimes trials, in the latter case by such methods as remission or reduction of sentences, provisional release and additional amenities. In Japan a review of sentences is long overdue.

Another advantage frequently claimed is that we have made it impossible for the Germans to say, as they said after the first World War, that ' we were never beaten, we were starved ' or, as some preferred ' we were stabbed in the back ', or again ' the Generals let the army down '. It would not have been worth while to incur all the casualties and losses of the last two years of the war to gain a safeguard against a similar excuse now. Such claims are something that can never be countered except by the nation itself. After the German Commander-in-Chief had himself proposed an armistice in 1918 and the Germans had had to submit to so harsh a Treaty one would hardly have thought that they could make such claims. And yet they did—and they will do it again. Already some Germans are saying: ' Hitler and the Nazis let Germany down ' and others that ' the Generals let Hitler down '!

Other Claims

To these lists of advantages wrongly claimed as having been gained at the War Crimes Trials there must be added some which are much more popular with lawyers, and especially British lawyers, than with laymen.

The first and most important of these is the establishment of a Rule of Law to do for nations what national systems of law have done for individuals throughout the world by providing for the punishment and prevention of crime and the maintenance of order.

No doubt that is a very high ideal and it is provided for by the structure of the Charter of the United Nations with the International Court of Justice at the Hague as its principal judicial organ, which *in theory* should even be able to clear up the legal aftermath of a war. *In practice*, however, if Victor States have committed the same crimes as those of which they accuse the enemy, if they have so much to hide that by one expedient or another they have to keep their misdeeds out of the jurisdiction of the Court, if they wish to dictate the list of crimes beforehand and to create them *ex post facto*, then that system becomes unusable. The United Nations simply cannot create a Tribunal or a system of Tribunals, as did the four principal Allies, to work on those lines. They would have to be fair to the two parties. In deciding on aggressions, for example, they would have to investigate the allegations and elicit the facts from both sides. Their Courts could not use captured documents of the Vanquished, even great documents of State, without obtaining the corresponding documents of the Victors. They would have to pay much more attention than did the

Nuremberg and Tokyo Tribunals to ' international custom, as evidence of a general practice accepted as law '.[1]   For example, they could not ignore the Universal Declaration of Human Rights approved by the General Assembly of the United Nations on December 10, 1948, and especially the following Articles:—

Article 10

Everyone is entitled in full equality to a fair and public hearing by *an independent and impartial Tribunal* in the determination of his rights and obligations and of any criminal charge against him.

Article 11

1.   Everyone charged with a penal offence has *the right to be presumed innocent until proved guilty* according to law in a public trial at which he has had all the guarantees necessary for his defence.

2.   *No one shall be held guilty of any penal offence on account of any act or omission which did not constitute a penal offence, under national or international law, at the time when it was committed.*[2] Nor shall a heavier penalty be imposed than the one that was applicable at the time the penal offence was committed.

It is inconceivable that the United Nations would consider a Tribunal composed exclusively of Victor judges to be ' an independent and impartial tribunal ' for the trial of the Van-quished as insisted upon by Article 10.   Similarly, Article 1 of the Charter of the Nuremberg Tribunal establishing it ' for the just and prompt trial and punishment of the major war criminals of the European Axis ' is hardly consistent with the principle enunciated in Article 11, 1.   And the *ex post facto* creation of crimes for the Nuremberg and Tokyo Tribunals is utterly incompatible with Article 11, 2.

In these circumstances the value of the Nuremberg and Tokyo trials for the establishment of a Rule of Law appears negligible.   Rather have they given it a grave setback.

[1] Statute of the International Court of Justice, Article 38 (b).
[2] Author's italics.

In this connection the following report of a recent speech by Lord Oaksey, who as Lord Justice Lawrence presided with so much distinction over the Nuremberg Tribunal, is of interest:—

' After the Nuremberg trial it seemed that the rules of law laid down there, would be recognized by all civilized nations. *Now it was doubtful whether that acceptance could be relied on.*[1] The Soviet Union appears to have abandoned the principle activating it in 1945. It may be there is some explanation of Russian diplomacy which we at present do not comprehend. It does not appear that there is any principle or practice that we can hope to rely on for the rule of law that must some day govern the world. It appears at present impossible to rely on the submission of all nations to a complete system of international law. The United Nations is trying to do something about it, but with so many checks and counter-checks and so many vetoes and counter-vetoes it is not safe to rely on the United Nations alone.'[2]

While agreeing that the Nuremberg (and for the matter of that the Tokyo) trials have failed to establish international confidence in any Rule of Law they sought to apply, many people will, with deference, disagree in attributing the blame entirely to Russia.

Victor Trials also, if not exactly commended, are strongly defended as fair by some high Legal Authorities.[3] Other advantages claimed are the inclusion in the Charters of new crimes *ex post facto*; and the laying down of the doctrine that the waging of aggressive war is a crime.

It is unnecessary to repeat here the arguments already advanced against these points. But, as a good many British

[1] Authors italics.

[2] *The Times*, June 21, 1949.

[3] A point on Victor trials that should be noted is the protest made to the Bulgarian Government by the British Minister at Sofia on September 25, 1947, against the execution of Mr. Nikola Petkov, Leader of the Bulgarian Agrarian Party and of the Parliamentary Opposition for anti-communist activities. One of the arguments he used was that ' the three judges of the Court and two State prosecutors were members of the Communist party.' We rightly protested against the trial and execution of Mr. Petkov by his political victor opponents : and yet, we were at the time taking part in a trial under similar conditions at Tokyo !

and American lawyers are known not to share the orthodox legal views, it may be of interest to quote a few brief extracts from the dissenting Judgement of Mr. Justice Pal, the representative of India, at the Tokyo trials. The whole passage is characterized by independence, lucidity, and learning; unfortunately, considerations of space forbid more than the following glimpse: ' But whatever the prosecution's view, in my opinion the criminality of the acts alleged must be determined with reference to the rules of international law existing at the date of the commission of the alleged acts (p. 26). . . . So far as the terms of the demand of (unconditional) surrender go there is nothing in them . . . which either expressly or by necessary implication would authorize the victor nation or the Supreme Command to legislate for Japan and for the Japanese in respect of crimes . . . (pp. 31–2). From what has been stated above it seems amply clear that *if the Allied Powers as victors have not, under international law, the legal right* to treat such persons as war criminals, they have not derived any such right by treaty or otherwise. The Allied Powers have nowhere given the slightest indication of their intention to assume any power which does not belong to them in law. It is, therefore, pertinent to inquire what is the extent *of the lawful authority of a victor* over the vanquished in international relations. . . . Apart from the right of reprisal, the victor would, no doubt, have the right of punishing persons who have violated the laws of war. But to say that the victor can define a crime at his will and then punish for that crime would be to revert back to those days when he was allowed to devastate the occupied country with fire and the sword, appropriate all public and private property therein and kill the inhabitants or take them away into captivity ' (pp. 31–2).

Again and again in the different sections of his dissenting Judgement Mr. Justice Pal insists that ' prisoners can be tried only for breaches of recognized laws of war ' (p. 53), and that it is beyond the rules of international law as they stand, for Victors to establish new crimes or new definitions, or to punish prisoners for having committed offences according to the new definitions (pp. 64, 68). He is also a consistent critic of Victor trials.

Mr. Justice Pal's contention has received powerful confirmation from the Universal Declaration of Human Rights approved by the General Assembly of the United Nations on December 10, 1948, Article 11, subsection 2, quoted above.

That pregnant Article appears to demolish, morally at any rate, the validity of a great part of the Nuremberg and Tokyo sentences, to render reconsideration absolutely essential.

Mr. Justice Pal on Aggressive Warfare

Turning to aggressive warfare Mr. Justice Pal tears to pieces the arguments in support of the theory that the framers of the Charter had the right to make it a war crime retrospectively or that the Tribunals were entitled to treat it as such. In that respect of course his general argument against their right to enunciate any *ex post facto* laws applies. In reply to the favourite argument that the Briand-Kellogg Pact of 1928 for the renunciation of war as an instrument of policy made aggressive war a crime, he points out that the Pact leaves intact the right of self-defence and that Mr. Kellogg himself in accepting it, made a declaration that ' *the right of self-defence was not limited to the defence of territory under the sovereignty of the state concerned*, and that under the treaty *each state would have the prerogative of judging for itself*, what action the right of self-defence covered, and when it came into play, subject only to the *risk* that the statement might not be endorsed by the rest of the world ' (Pal. p. 90). He also mentions a corresponding British reservation, freedom of action in defence of the Dominions and Colonies.

France made a corresponding reservation in respect of her national defence. It is clear then, says Mr. Pal, that the parties only intended the pact as a contractual obligation—an obligation ' *dependent on the will of the states*, in as much as it is left to these states to determine whether the action was or was not a violation of the obligation undertaken by the pact ' (p. 91).

Mr. Pal also insists that considerations relevant for the determination of the *legal* character of rules of conduct are— *first* ' final ascertainment by agencies other than parties to the disputes ', *i.e.* not by the Victors as at Nuremberg and Tokyo. He quotes various authorities in support of his thesis and reaches the conclusion: ' That the pre-existing legal position of war in international life remained unaffected. The only effect produced by the Pact is the *possible influencing of world opinion* against the offending belligerent and thereby developing the law to abiding sentiment between States . . .' (p. 107).

In reply to a contention that aggression, being a war which is not waged in self-defence, cannot be justified and is consequently a crime, Mr. Pal observes that 'the question what is a war in self-defence was left to be determined by each party '(p. 109). Later he hits the nail on the head with the observation, ' When the conduct of the nations is taken into account the law will perhaps be found to be that *only a lost war is a crime* ' (p. 128).

That is in line with Field-Marshal Viscount Montgomery's statement that ' the Nuremberg trials made the waging of unsuccessful war a crime, for the Generals of the defeated side would be tried and then hanged.'

Similarly, Mr. Pal disposes of the various resolutions of the League of Nations which condemned aggression by pointing out that the League of Nations was not a law-making body. ' It was simply a system of co-operation,' a contention which is supported by the Preamble to the Covenant.

Summing up, after many more pertinent passages that I am loath to omit, Mr. Pal says: ' *In my judgement* no category of war became a crime in international life up to the date of commencement of the world war under our consideration. Any distinction between just and unjust war remains only in the theory of the international legal philosophers. The Pact of Paris did not affect the character of war and failed to introduce any criminal responsibility in respect of any category of war in international life. No customary law developed so as to make any war a crime. . . . The Moscow Declaration of 1943 merely expresses the will of the Victors; and its product, the Charter, cannot bring a new law into being, especially an *ex post facto* development in condemning the long and past acts of the accused " (pp. 152–3).

A more devastating criticism it would be hard to conceive.

I have no doubt at all that Mr. Justice Pal is absolutely right. As one who was cognisant of all that went on in connection with the making of the Kellogg Pact, of which I was an enthusiastic supporter, and as one with special responsibilities at all stages in the co-ordination of planning and all that affected it between the wars, I assert that from the signature of the pact until I read the Nuremberg Judgement and sentences, I never heard a hint that it could be used as the basis of a war crimes charge of planning, preparing, or waging war. At the London Conference of June, 1945, M. Gros (for France) repeatedly rebutted the claim that aggression could be made a criminal charge against individuals.

The Influence of Russian Judges

In the course of his long and detailed examination of the group of subjects discussed above as being among the achievements claimed for the Nuremberg Tribunal, Mr. Pal makes the following astute observation: ' Questions of law are not decided in an intellectual quarantine area in which legal doctrine and the local history of the dispute alone are retained and all else forcibly excluded. We cannot afford to be ignorant of the world in which disputes arise ' (Pal, p. 226). Yet, that is just what the Nuremberg and Tokyo Tribunals were forced to do owing to the presence on the bench of a Russian Judge. They had to consider the unquestionable and undisputed aggressions of Germany and Japan and to issue their judgements thereon without any reference to the corresponding and almost simultaneous major acts of aggressions committed by the U.S.S.R. This is so important a factor bearing on the questions of whether these trials ought to have been held; whether they were fair trials; and whether such a procedure ought ever to be repeated in the future, that I have kept it back deliberately until now.

The subject can best be seen against a summary of the development of the policy of the Soviet Union up to the outbreak of war. I am basing myself on a close study of Mr. Stalin's *Problems of Leninism*.

Marshal Stalin's ' MEIN KAMPF '

" In every country people are asking why the Russians, who were such wonderful allies in the war, are not co-operating better in peace. The key to the puzzle lies in Stalin's book, *Problems of Leninism*, a translation of the Russian eleventh edition published in Moscow in 1945. This work has been described as Stalin's *Mein Kampf*, and, as the Nuremberg Judgement said of Hitler's prototype, its importance ' lies in the unmistakable attitude of aggression revealed throughout its pages '; but with this difference, that Stalin's aggression is ideological rather than military.

" Nevertheless, the book is disturbing. In 642 ponderous pages of lectures, speeches, and writings is told the story of the Russian Revolution, its basic theories, aims and plans, its trials and troubles, and the strategy and tactics by which they were overcome. There is much use of military terminology. Marx and Lenin are quoted as holy writ. Humour is rare, but there are digs at Mr. Churchill's ' march of the fourteen States '.

" Only once does Stalin let himself go when, almost in Hitler's vein, he denounces ' the Trotsky-Bukharin bunch of spies, assassins, and wreckers who kow-towed to the foreign world ', and two batches of ' fiends ' who were sentenced to be shot in 1937 and 1938 respectively. The Dictatorship of the Proletariat, like the Fascist and Nazi Dictatorships, has its blood baths and purges.

" Stalin envisages the revolution in three phases. The first two cover the period from its inception in 1903 until October 1917, when Tsarism and Imperialism were overthrown and the Communist Dictatorship established. The third stage, from 1917 onwards, was devoted to the consolidation of the new régime and its development *as a base for the overthrow of imperialism in all countries*. That process is still unfinished, but it is an integral part of Lenin's lay-out, as shown by the following: ' The overthrow of the power of the bourgeoisie and establishment of the power of the proletariat in one country does not mean that the complete victory of Socialism has been ensured. . . . The victory of the revolution *in at least several countries* is needed.' In Lenin's subsequent passages the words in italics become ' in all countries '.

" This was no short-range policy. Lenin described it as ' an entire historical epoch ', and Stalin adds: ' replete with civil wars and external conflicts, with persistent organizational work and economic construction, with advances and retreats, victories and defeats.' Marx was even more explicit. ' You will have to go through fifteen, twenty, fifty years of civil wars and international conflicts . . .'—not a cheerful prospect!

" Simultaneous support to revolution everywhere at once was rejected from the first. There must be discrimination with first priority to proletarian revolutions. But aid to other national movements, if revolutionary in character, was not banned. The decision depended ' on the actual results obtained as shown by the general balance sheet of the struggle against imperialism '. Thus in 1924 Stalin described ' the struggle the Egyptian merchants and bourgeois intellectuals are waging for the independence of Egypt ' as ' objectively a *revolutionary* struggle '. Every step along the road to liberation in India and China was ' a steam-hammer blow at imperialism '. In 1927 he boasted: ' Having sown the seeds of revolution both in the centre of imperialism as well as in its rear, having weakened the might of imperialism in the mother countries and having shaken its domination in the colonies, the October Revolution has thereby jeopardized the very existence of world capitalism as a whole.' Although these claims were completely refuted by war experience, they provide a useful warning.

" Social democrat politicians come in for much abuse. After quoting Lenin's denunciation of them as ' the labour lieutenants of the capitalist class ', Stalin observes: ' It is impossible to put an end to capitalism without putting an end to Social-Democraticism in the labour movement.'

" Setbacks to the attack on capitalism were foreseen and provided for. The principle was that strategy within a given stage of the struggle remains constant, but ' tactics change according to the flow and ebb '. In particular ' retreats ' were prescribed ' to gain time to demoralize the enemy, and to accumulate forces in order to resume the offensive '. These tactics were used frequently in the internal struggle with peasants and bourgeoise, *e.g.* the NEP (new economic policy of 1921) is mentioned as a temporary retreat.

" In foreign affairs Stalin describes the Brest-Litovsk Treaty as ' a model of this strategy '. The non-aggression pacts with Finland, Poland, and Rumania furnish later examples. The object of these treaties was to gain time, and they were callously broken when convenient. No doubt the Agreement of August, 1939, with Hitler was another ' tactical deviation '. It gave Russia the Baltic States and half Poland.

" That brief summary shows why, fundamentally, co-operation with Russia is difficult. There is no sign that her policy has changed. Were that the case Stalin's book would hardly have been published in 1945. The Russian domination of Eastern Europe and the installation of Communist Governments are consistent with Lenin's insistence on 'the victory of the revolution in at least several countries'. The attempt to hem in Turkey from East and West, linked with the reopening of the question of the Straits, although followed by a tactical retreat in Persia with prospects of another in Greece, suggests that revolution 'in all countries' is still in the programme. So, even more, do the Communist activities in Albania, Italy, France, and Spain.

" For the moment the risk of war is slight, owing to economic exhaustion. But on a long view the situation is dangerous, for ideological aggression, if persisted in, will lead to war. Clearly we and our friends must not neglect our armaments.

" But we must try to disperse the storm clouds. There are deep-rooted Russian suspicions to be dispelled about our support of the counter-revolution in 1918–19, the atomic bomb, and so forth. Then Russia has to be convinced that she has nothing to fear from the so-called 'capitalist' Powers, so long as she leaves other countries alone; but it must be made unmistakably clear that all forms of external aggression will be countered everywhere by deeds as well as words, as in Greece to-day. That will take time, and will need truth, toughness, tact, persistence and patience, all qualities which Mr. Bevin possesses in abundance." [1]

We must recall the dates which tell the story of the first German and Russian aggressions in 1939–40. The Russo-German Pact of Neutrality and non-Aggression was signed on August 23, 1939, behind the back of an Anglo-French Military Mission, which was trying to negotiate a military pact with Marshal Voroshilov. The secret Protocol affirming *inter alia* Russia's special interest in Bessarabia was signed on the same day. The German aggression on Poland began on September 1, 1939, and the Russian aggression on September 17, 1939, after most of the Polish troops had been drawn off to oppose the German invasion. On September 27 a second secret protocol was signed allowing the Soviet to take over Lithuania and

---

[1] I published this in the *Sunday Times* on April 27, 1947, and reproduce it here with the permission of its Editor.

settling the partition of Poland.[1]   On November 30, 1939, the Russians, notwithstanding their pact of non-aggression and neutrality of January, 1932, invaded Finland, and on December 13, 1939, the League of Nations Assembly denounced the invasion as a breach of the Kellogg Pact.   In June, 1940, Russia occupied, and in August, 1940, she annexed, the Baltic States with all of whom she had concluded many Pacts of neutrality and non-aggression in the 20's and 30's, right up to 1939.   Meanwhile, Germany had attacked Norway and Denmark, April 9, 1940, Holland, Belgium, and Luxemburg, May 10, 1940, and France a few days later, and Great Britain had mined the Norway Leads, April 8, 1940, and had landed forces in Norway (about April 15).   Broadly then the Russian aggressions in the east were proceeding more or less simultaneously with the German aggressions and the counter-operations of the Allies in the West.

The fruits of the earlier Russian aggressions were fully harvested in 1947, after the Nuremberg trials were over, and are still not widely appreciated in Western Europe.   To quote Dr. F. W. Pick:—

' Russia has gained a common frontier with Norway and robbed Finland of its only northern outlet, thus throwing her fully back on to the Baltic. . . . Finland, through the Peace Treaty of 1947, is burdened with heavy reparations and serious losses of national territory.   Estonia, Latvia, Lithuania, and half of former East Prussia have been declared Russian territory, thus making Pillau the Western naval fortress of the Soviet Union.   In addition, as long as Poland—now with its broad access to the sea, a major Baltic power—is under Soviet influence that sea has almost become a Russian lake. . . . Are we then back—say in the eighteenth century ? ' [2]

This is the complete replica, in the case of Russia, of the Nazi acts of aggression—the plot and schemes, principles, and policy, preparations, strategy, tactics, and actual execution, most of it planned long before the Nazi movement was born or thought of, carried out before the beginning of the Nuremberg and Tokyo Trials, and continued concurrently with the trials and ever since to this very day!

---

[1] James F. Byrnes, *Speaking Frankly*, p. 286.

[2] F. W. Pick, *Contemporary History*. ' The Baltic Tug of War ', p. 249.

Soviet Susceptibilities

How was it that the Russians were allowed to participate in the prosecution of Germany on charges of aggression when the League had denounced her as an aggressor ? Why was it that the Nazi defence at Nuremberg was not allowed to refer to these acts of Russian aggression ? Had they been permitted to do so, had the Tribunal not worked in intellectual quarantine, it must have seen that in the sphere of aggression the Nazis had only been doing what Russia had done with complete impunity. Surely none of the prisoners could have been condemned on the political charges if the Tribunal had been able to take official cognizance of these contemporary Russian aggressions.

Mr. John Wheeler-Bennett in his *Munich: Prologue to Tragedy*,[1] writing of the Russo-German Agreement of August 23, 1939, gives the explanation: ' *In deference to Soviet susceptibilities the protocols were not introduced as evidence*[2] before the International Military Tribunal at Nuremberg, but Baron von Weizsäcker, the former State Secretary to the German Foreign Ministry, was permitted to refer to their contents under cross-examination on May 21, 1946,' though only from memory.

The phrase ' deference to Soviet susceptibilities ' accounts for a great deal. It explains why the London Charter-making Conference in 1945 was so anxious to prevent the defendants from putting forward the kind of defence which it was known from captured documents was their one chance, and which would have been so terribly inconvenient to the Allies. It explains why it was impossible to have a neutral tribunal, or even to include a few neutrals to sit with the victor judges. It explains why the Tribunals had to work in quarantine and to rule out as irrelevant anything that might incriminate an allied subject, or indeed anything not bearing directly on the selected, immediate charges. It explains why they had to dodge the fact that acts of aggression—as committed by Russia after the Kellogg Pact had supposedly created a new law—had remained as they have always been, the practice of mankind. However reprehensible, it had never been charged as a crime against any individual. It explains why so many

---

[1] p. 412, Footnote.   [2] Author's italics.

people are saying to-day that there is only one war crime—and
that is, to be on the losing side! ' Deference to Soviet susceptibilities ' perhaps explains why at the Tokyo trial Mr. Shigemitsu, who had been struck out by the Chief Prosecutor from the
list of persons to be charged, was reinstated in the list shortly
after the arrival of the Russian Judge. Perhaps it also explains
the following passage in a progress report presented by the Chief
Prosecutor to the American President on June 6, 1945:—

' These hearings, however, must not be regarded in the same
light as a trial under our system, where defence is a matter of
constitutional right. Fair hearings for the accused are, of
course, required to make sure that we punish only the right
men for the right reasons. But the procedure of these hearings
may properly bar obstruction and dilatory tactics resorted to
by defendants in our ordinary criminal trials.' [1]

The balance, then, may be struck. On the one hand, we
have to set whatever we think remains of the advantages
claimed for the War Crimes Trials after the criticism to which
they have been exposed, viz.—the framing of the Charter; the
Power of the Precedent; a workable Precedent for International Trials; Compilation of a documentation of Nazi
activities to stop Nazi hero-worship and martyrdoms ; Up-
rooting of National Socialism; the Germans can never say
' We were not beaten '; the creation of new crimes ex post facto,
including Aggression.

On the other side, we have the counter-claims, viz.:—War
Crimes Trials were part of a most unfortunate policy of threats,
which exacerbated the war; forced a fight to a finish; gave
the enemy the courage of despair; strengthened Hitler and
the propaganda of Goebbels; rendered impossible peace over-
tures or negotiations; lengthened the war; rendered Treaty-
making and German reconstruction after the war almost
impossible; bled the whole world white; and weakened the
moral position of the allies. To these political criticisms must be
added: misgivings about the London Conference of June, 1945,
to draft the Charter; the exclusion from the trials of subjects
important to the defence such as the Russian aggressions;
indefensibility of trials by the Victors of the Vanquished; also

[1] The International Conference on Military Trials, London, 1945, Paper
LXIII, p. 46.

of new *ex post facto* crimes including Aggression; the handicap
to the defendants of the unavoidable ' deference to Soviet
susceptibilities '; the points advanced in the protest of American
Counsel for defence against the unfairness of the Tokyo trials;
the absence of British Counsel for the defence from both trials;
the inordinate length of the indictments.

Every reader can judge for himself whether the War Crimes
Trials in these circumstances could possibly have reached the
standard of justice and fairness fit and proper for the judgement
of statesmen of the highest rank, Admirals, Generals, Air
Marshals, or their equivalent, diplomats, high civil servants,
and other national leaders—or anyone else! Remembering
that it was a Victors' trial does anyone think that the results
are likely to be accepted as fair by the British, allied, neutral,
and ex-enemy peoples now and down the ages ? And, finally,
would anybody, even if confident of innocence, if placed in the
position of a defeated enemy, feel that a fair deal could be
counted on from a similar Court created by an enemy after a
victorious war ? Would anyone entrust to such a Court, with
a Charter laid down for it by the victorious enemy, with power
to create and interpret new *ex post facto* crimes, the fate of himself or herself, of a husband or wife, or sweetheart, son or
daughter, parent, near relation, or friend ? ·

The Future

One of the main objects of this book has been fulfilled,
namely, to compile, for the benefit of history, material to show
that policies based on unworthy motives such as unconditional
surrender and war crimes trials do not pay and should never
be announced in the middle stages of a major war.

It has been a grim story to tell but there is no reason why it
should not have a good ending. In fact, in the case of Unconditional Surrender a good ending has already been reached,
thanks to Mr. Bevin. The Foreign Secretary by telling the
truth in the plain and simple language quoted on page 51 has
virtually closed that episode. He has shown that the War
Cabinet was not consulted, that if they had been consulted they
would not have agreed to Unconditional Surrender, that in the
welter of war they accepted responsibility for their leader's

decision, and that the post-war results were as bad as one would expect. Mr. Churchill has confirmed Mr. Bevin's statement about the probable views of his Cabinet, and has shown that unconditional surrender was not a plan of his choosing, but that he felt obliged to accept it and carried it out loyally as a good colleague to its proposer. The main difference between the two is that Mr. Churchill takes a less dim view than Mr. Bevin of the results of unconditional surrender, but here Mr. Bevin is the responsible Minister immediately affected.

In these circumstances it seems unlikely that a policy of unconditional surrender is likely ever again to be adopted in the middle of a major war and Mr. Bevin may have rendered a great and lasting service to mankind.

It remains to clear up the other great branch of the subject, namely, War Crimes Trials, in an equally satisfactory way. That is more complicated and more difficult.

On that, as already stated, I have confined myself almost entirely to the trials of political charges such as planning, preparing, and waging wars of aggression, and have left the trials of conventional war crimes to others. A vast amount of material on both aspects has been accumulated in the books mentioned in the Introduction.

So far as the British and American Governments are concerned a good deal has already been done to give satisfaction on this aspect of the question. The Nuremberg and Tokyo Trials of the more important of the accused came to an end many months ago. In the British and American Zones of Germany the secondary trials which, however, included very high officers and officials will probably be completed by the end of the year. A gradual review is being undertaken of earlier sentences, but the number of cases is very large and the process must be very slow.

In Japan also the trials are believed to have come to an end.

That is all satisfactory as far as it goes, but more is required before the spirit of bitterness which these trials have engendered is removed. Each of the 15,000 sentences imposed in the British Zone remains a centre of bitterness against the Allies in general, and Great Britain in particular. The same thing has happened in the other Zones. Can anyone be surprised at the nationalism displayed during the German Elections in the summer of 1949 ? Reconsideration of such huge numbers must be a long business. In bringing their own trials to an end the British and American Governments have handed over a number of cases to the Germans and so long as the German Trials continue they also will be creating foci of bitterness. In Japan also, as more than once mentioned, the cases of Shigemitsu and Togo and other survivors clamour for reconsideration.

There is only one remedy to bring all this shame, misery, and wretchedness to an end, and that is amnesty. Probably it will be said that other nations make that too difficult. If that is so we and the Americans should undertake it wherever we have the power.

We might agree on an amnesty day on which we would release all prisoners convicted of war crimes other than sheer sadism, and those awaiting trial. Perhaps the amnesty day might fall on the same day as the old Armistice Day. But instead of it being a Day of Remembrance it would be a Day of Oblivion when prisoners would be released and reunited to their families and the politics, trials, and errors of the war would be effaced for evermore. Even unilateral action by ourselves, or bilateral action with America would probably be followed by other nations. But how much better if the United Nations, or if the Russian complication makes that impossible, the Council of Europe and its Consultative Assembly could launch the scheme at once. That would strike the imagination of all mankind, and do much to exorcise the war spirit. It would also be a decisive step towards peace.

INDEX

147